Austin McClee

ERIC VENABLE

A TALE OF TWO YOUTH WORKERS

A YOUTH MINISTRY FABLE

ZONDERVAN®

ZONDERVAN.com/
AUTHORTRACKER
follow your favorite authors

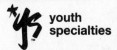
youth
specialties

YOUTH SPECIALTIES

A Tale of Two Youth Workers: A Youth Ministry Fable
Copyright 2009 by Eric Venable

Youth Specialties resources, 300 S. Pierce St., El Cajon, CA 92020 are published by Zondervan, 5300 Patterson Ave. SE, Grand Rapids, MI 49530.

Library of Congress Cataloging-in-Publication Data

Venable, Eric.
 A tale of two youth workers : a youth ministry fable / Eric Venable.
    p. cm.
 Includes bibliographical references and index.
 ISBN 978-0-310-28524-3 (hardcover : alk. paper)
 1. Church work with youth. I. Title.
 BV4447.V46 2009

 259'.23—dc22   2009009692

Cover design by Toolbox Studios
Interior design by SharpSeven Design

Printed in the United States of America

---

09 10 11 12 13 14 • 18 17 16 15 14 13 12 11 10 9 8 7 6 5 4 3 2 1

For Pamela, Audrey, and Catherine—

You show me Jesus every day.

CONTENTS

FOREWORD

Eric Venable has a giant heart for young people. Or maybe a better way to put it is that Eric Venable IS a giant heart for young people, walking around in a normal-looking body.

Relatively normal-looking.

I got to watch firsthand, because we got to work together in the same church. And I saw the way his heart would beat and his mind would race when he thought about God and students and how to help students come to know the God who loves them so. I heard parents express a level of appreciation for what Eric had done in their children's lives that was off the chart.

And now you get to read some—not just from Eric's heart—but also from Eric's head. He's put some of his key observations into an easy-to-read parable form. You will learn from these pages the role that doubt plays in the spiritual formation of a young life. I don't know how any person could grow up in our world without being inundated by questions. But where do they take them? Too often the world in general exalts doubt and discounts faith. (How often we hear the phrases, "honest doubt" and "blind faith," without thinking about how doubt can also be blind and faith can also be honest.) But too often the church is not a safe place for doubters.

So Eric walks beside anyone who desires to help guide young people through the valley of doubt, into a faith that is authentic and life-giving. The main gift needed is not a toolkit full of answers. The main gift needed is love. Because the wonderful thing about doing God's work with young people is that God is the main one doing the work! That, says Eric, takes loads of pressure off the human being involved. We help create an environment through honesty and caring and acceptance and encouragement. But in the midst of the chaos and the mess of growing up, it's God who does the growth production.

So open these pages, and learn from a master of youth work. And from the Master who first thought up youth.

Then get to work.

John Ortberg

ACKNOWLEDGMENTS

Special thanks to—

Mom—Your love and faith hold me tight.

Dad—Thanks for believing in me and listening to all my stories.

Mark and Cari—Thanks for always letting me be the goofy little brother.

Bob, Brian, and Michael—Your friendship has been life-giving.

Britt and Mel—You are wonderful.

Kurt, Marko, Nate, Scott, Johnny, Andy, Heather, Alan, John, April, Jim, Ken, Corrie, Steve, Sean, Phil, Jason, and everyone from the Middle School Summit—Thanks for your friendship, insight, and encouragement.

Charley, Stew, Dusty, Ryan, Brian, Melissa, Michelle, Lyndy, Jared, Annie, Becky, Bonnie, and li'l Kelley—I had as much fun as Richard Simmons, David Hasselhoff, and Sally Struthers' bonus pants!

The good people of Menlo Park Presbyterian Church and Emmanuel Faith Church—Thanks for allowing me the privilege of ministering with you.

And Doug—Brrriiiiiiaagggggggghh!

CHAPTER 1
A NEW BEGINNING

The phone rang, but Wes was in screening mode, content to let caller I.D. do its job.

"Call from...Coastline Commu," the digital voice announced.

Coastline Community Church.

Wes' heart tap-danced in his chest.

It was the call he'd been waiting for—he just didn't think it would come so soon. Wes sat back in his chair and took a deep breath as he picked up the phone.

Don't be nervous, he told himself. *It's only the most important conversation of your career. You know—the one that could change your life forever. No big deal.*

"Good morning, Wes," a deep voice greeted him. The voice belonged to Richard, the senior pastor of Coastline Community Church, the largest church in the denomination. "How do you feel about moving to California?"

Wes opened his mouth, but no sound came out. That wasn't the question he was expecting. He and Jenny had just returned from a visit to Coastline. He was expecting to field some additional questions about his age and experience—the one area in the interview where Wes had felt vulnerable. Jenny said he'd covered well, but that didn't ease his unease.

He kept asking himself, *Would a church the size of Coastline really turn over its youth ministry to a guy younger than 30 with only one church stay under his belt*?

Apparently the answer was *yes*.

"Umm, yeah," Wes replied. "I think I'd really like that. But I didn't think you'd just come out and ask that. I thought you might have more questions for me."

"Well, I like to cut to the chase, Wes," Richard explained. "We have a huge need, and you're the guy to fill our leadership void. We see your skill set and gifts, and they line up exactly with what we're looking for. The search committee and pastors were unanimous. We think you'll fit in great here. So why wait?"

Wes caught his breath and tried to slow his runaway heartbeat. *Sound professional,* he told himself.

"I'll have to discuss this with Jenny," he said. "We've been talking about it, and I think she's excited...um...*open* to the possibility. I would also love an offer letter so the details are clear to everyone. You know, some stuff on paper."

Wes kicked himself. *Stuff*? *Who says* stuff?

Richard assured Wes that Coastline's COO would email an offer letter to him within 48 hours. "Look it over, pray it over, and let's talk more," he said.

"Richard, what are you thinking timewise?" Wes asked.

"The sooner, the better, Wes," Richard replied. "So whatever it takes to expedite the process, let us know. We want this to be as quick and smooth as possible. Here's my private number, Wes. Give me a call anytime as you think through this decision."

As soon as Wes hung up, he bellowed, "Yeah! Sweet action!"

Then he called Jenny at work.

"Are you sitting down?" he asked. "I just got off the phone with Richard from *the* Coastline Community Church. They're sending me an offer letter."

"Oh, my...just like that?" Jenny asked.

"Just like that?" Wes shot back. "You know God is in this. This is *exactly* what we've been praying for!"

"I don't remember you getting this excited when you got an offer from that church in Kansas City," Jenny said.

"And there's a perfectly good reason for that," Wes replied.

"It was in Kansas City," they said in unison.

"That would have been a lateral move," Wes explained. "But this—"

"This is big, isn't it?" Jenny said.

"Huge," Wes replied. "You were there. You saw it. You *felt* it. This is a church that gets youth ministry. And it's a church that thinks big. If something works, the whole church backs it. They don't make you beg for extra staff members when your youth ministry's bursting at the seams and tell you they need the money in your budget for more pressing issues."

"Are you saying you're not going to miss First Church?" Jenny asked.

"I'll miss the kids," Wes said.

"What about the staff?"

"I'll miss the youth group volunteers," Wes answered.

"What about life in Lansing—the joy of being a Michigander?" Jenny pressed.

"I'll miss the kids and the volunteers," Wes repeated. "Jenny, I can't tell you how excited I am. I keep thinking about what everyone told us in California."

"That we were the palest people they'd ever seen?"

"No," Wes said, "that the church releases its people to do ministry, and the job is as big as we want it to be."

"Does the same go for salary?" Jenny asked.

"Richard didn't give me a number, but I'm sure it'll be a big increase," Wes said.

"It'll have to be if we're going to afford California living," Jenny added.

"So tell me, Jenny, are you ready to sell your winter clothes?"

"Yes!" Jenny exclaimed.

"Are you going to miss scraping ice off your car windows?"

"Are you kidding?" Jenny asked.

"Will you miss the 'seasons'?"

"Heck, no!" Jenny said. "To be honest, honey, I never really liked the seasons. Very rude. They're all about themselves."

She paused.

"Wes, I can't work! I'll take my lunch break early. There's just so much to think about."

"Sounds great," Wes replied. "Where can we grab lunch at 10:45 a.m.?"

Life was exciting and busy for the first few months in California. Finding a place to live, establishing new relationships, and getting up to speed in the ministry gave Wes and Jenny a thrilling sense of momentum. They felt like they'd *arrived*.

One of the first things they did was establish a routine of talking about the new position every morning at a favorite coffeehouse. One morning Wes arrived before Jenny, who'd gotten a late start on her morning run.

Wes' brain was a whirl of activity. The potential before him excited and energized him. He repeated the Coastline mantra to himself: *The ministry's as big as you want it to be.*

Tiny butterflies fluttered in his stomach as he made a mental checklist of the things he no longer had to worry about:

- outgrowing building space
- seeing the words "too ambitious" written on his annual review
- negotiating with the ladies of Quilting for Christ for use of the multipurpose room

- having to explain to his unhappy pastor why an outreach event drew more kids than expected

Wes smiled broadly. *The ministry's as big as you want it to be,* he repeated.

The ministry's as big as you want it to be!

"The ministry's as big as you want it to be!"

"THE MINISTRY'S AS BIG AS YOU WANT IT TO BE!"

Wes glanced around the coffee shop. The woman at the table next to him was discreetly moving her chair away from him. Next to her was a mother who was whispering to her young daughter not to stare at "that man." Behind the counter a young barista was subtly motioning for the manager and nodding toward Wes.

Wes chuckled as he realized his interior monologue had gone verbal—again. He shook his head and offered a quick wave to the group—the universal sign for "I'm just an overexcited youth pastor and not a weapon-concealing escapee arguing with the demons in my head."

Memo to self, he thought. *Start wearing a Bluetooth headset so people assume you're having a conversation with someone else.*

When Jenny walked in Wes pulled her aside and quietly told her what had happened. She gave him a small smile before suddenly pulling away from him.

"No, I *don't* want to hear about any alien invasion!" she said, just loud enough for everyone in the place to hear. "Please, leave me alone!" She walked quickly to a table on the other side of the coffeehouse and sat down.

With a big grin on her face.

Every person in the shop suspiciously eyed Wes as he made his way over to her table and sat down.

"Hi, honey!" Jenny said brightly. "How's your morning?" She then pulled out her notebook and waited for Wes to start brainstorming. Taking notes was Jenny's way of framing their rambling coffee times. She gave shape to Wes' ideas and helped him create a consolidated plan and focus his energy.

Usually the list looked something like this:

- *Figure out greater church staff expectation.*
- *Take full-time student staff away for overnight.*
- *Meet with every youth leader a number of times in different contexts. (Schedule every meal!!!)*
- *Hang out with as many students as possible. Find the most influential—win them.*
- *Meet with other youth pastors in area. Get insight into schools and find out what they're doing.*
- *Change the existing program—just slightly—to show ownership and mix things up a bit.*

Jenny's notes gave Wes the grounding he needed during the whirlwind that was the first few months at Coastline. Wes ran on adrenaline and Starbucks, going from meeting to service to event and back again. He embraced the rush like a candy-crazed kid running house to house at Halloween.

The church offices were always abuzz with activity. And the loudest buzz usually came from the youth offices, much to the delight of the extroverted Wes. The constant interaction energized him, but it also added to his days in ways he'd never experienced. Wes would come into the office with what seemed like a light day only to find his schedule completely booked by noon.

Wes had shared an administrative assistant at his previous church. But at Coastline he had his own, as well as two others dedicated entirely to student ministry. He quickly learned to screen calls and appointments through his admin Bonnie, whom Jenny referred to as his "work wife."

Bonnie served as Wes' jungle guide through the Amazon of parents, people, and staff. She helped him learn to spot nuances he was blind to during his first few months on the job. She guarded him from the highly needy and welcomed the wonderful. Wes had no idea how many fires Bonnie put out. But he quickly recognized how easily many events ran because of Bonnie's ability to navigate—and follow up with leaders and parents.

All the usual firsts went well for Wes: The first leaders' meeting, the first parents' meeting, and the first big event. The youth group was all he'd hoped it would be. It was large, loud, and full of energy! Wes loved teaching in a room full of students. In turn, they seemed to like his vibe and personality. Having a full-time staff allowed him to do what he did best—be a leader—and freed him from having to worry about every detail and talk.

He knew he wasn't in Michigan anymore when the first weekend retreat filled up without much pushing.

"This is the first time in my youth ministry career that I'll be able to start a retreat without being exhausted from running around the week before," he told Jenny the night before the retreat. "I *love* this church!"

Wes tried hard not to verbally erupt at the Tuesday-morning pastors' meeting following the retreat. When his chance to talk came, he reported the best stories from the retreat and then casually declared that the youth group would most likely have to find a larger camp for its retreats. Wes played it off as simply a mathematical conclusion, but he felt like screaming it.

Richard, the senior pastor, caught Wes briefly in the hallway after the meeting.

"Keep thinking big, Wes!" he said. "I like where you're going."

Wes thanked Richard before adding some fuel to the fire.

"I think we should never stop dreaming about what God would have us be here," he said enthusiastically. "Imagine if we were to reach just 10 percent of the students in our community. We might have to buy our own camp!"

Richard smiled.

CHAPTER 3
FEEL FREE TO SUCCEED

Wes turned his key upside down and tried the lock again.

Still wouldn't fit.

What in the world? he thought.

He stepped off the porch and looked at the neighboring houses just to make sure he was at the right address. It was his house, all right. He'd know that overgrown shrubbery anywhere, even in the dark.

He returned to the door and held his keychain next to the porch light. They were his keys, all right. He tried again, but still couldn't get the key to fit. *Think,* he commanded himself. *Did Jenny say anything about having the locks changed?*

And that's when reality hit him with a quick jab between the eyes.

It's the church key, he realized. *My first instinct was to grab the church key. Jenny is gonna love that.*

He found the right key and let himself in as quietly as he could. The only light in the house was the flickering glow of the TV in the family room. He tiptoed down the hall, negotiating the still-unpacked boxes of seminary notes and leadership books.

Jenny, a morning person, could fall asleep any time in the evening if she was alone. All bets were off past nine o'clock. The clock in the kitchen flashed 10:47 p.m. Wes was determined not to wake her.

"Turn on a light before you break your neck," Jenny called from the couch.

"That's okay," Wes replied. "I've got the route memorized."

"It's no wonder," Jenny said. "This is the third night this week. I thought you said you were going to start dialing things back."

"The problem is no one told the church," he said. "I'm just feeling this tremendous pressure to be at every church meeting and youth program. I think it's expected of me—at least until I establish myself. We have to remember—"

"Big church programs don't happen without involved leaders," Jenny completed his thought. "I've heard that song before."

"I promise I'll pull back and start saying no after I establish my leadership," Wes said.

"How will you know when that happens?" Jenny asked. "Do you get a T-shirt or lapel pin that says 'leadership established'?"

"No, no, Jenny, it's not like that," Wes explained with a grin. "Here you get a sash to wear around on Sunday mornings, just like pageant queens! I'm shooting for the Hybels or Stanley sash! A kid can dream, you know?"

"What about the Rick Warren Leadership Sash?" Jenny asked.

"Unattainable without a book deal," Wes replied. "Besides, it's a fruity tropical pattern!"

"But you really are going to start slowing down, aren't you?" Jenny asked.

This time there was no playfulness in her voice.

"Absolutely," Wes said. "I just need to get past Sunday. I have to make sure my first official appearance in the 'big church' goes well. They take that stuff very seriously here."

Thursday afternoon's walk-through was even more detailed than Wes had imagined. He spent the first 20 minutes just talking with the sound guys about microphone placement and handling.

Whoa! Wes thought to himself five minutes in. *You're playing in the major leagues now, slugger.*

Charlie, the chief sound guy, fixed Wes with an intense gaze as he explained the dos and don'ts of wireless mics. Wes tried to maintain eye contact with Charlie, but found his eyes wandering to the top of the soundman's head, where Charlie's hairline was staging a cowardly retreat from the front.

Don't even start thinking about it, Wes told himself. *Stay focused. This is important.*

"The one thing you *don't* want to do—" Charlie began.

Wes glanced up again at Charlie's dome. *Those little stragglers at the top look like guitar strings,* he noted. *I wonder if they're trying to put the band back together.* He bit the inside of his cheeks to keep from grinning, and reestablished eye contact with Charlie.

The soundman continued his well-practiced instructions. "If you get onstage and find that your mic isn't working, make sure you—"

I could use Charlie's hair as a "bridge to life" illustration, Wes thought. *I could get close-up footage and use it with the middle schoolers to show how Jesus is the bridge to life. Or, better yet, I could bring Charlie up on stage and do it live!*

"Any questions?" Charlie asked.

Yeah, I was wondering if I could borrow you and your comb-over some Wednesday evening, Wes thought. But in a rare victory for his brain over his mouth, Wes didn't say it. He just smiled at Charlie and said, "No, I think I'm ready to go."

The walk-through itself was quick and surprisingly intense. Wes had never noticed the markers on the stage that showed people where to stand. But there were a number of them—too many for Wes' comfort.

Jared, the worship arts pastor, led the walk-through like an overcaffeinated auctioneer. Wes struggled to write down his cues—when to start walking to the stage, where to stand, how much time to spend on each announcement, what to cover in his prayer.

Wes tried to keep a calm demeanor even as he became lost in the torrent of Jared's instructions. He breathed a silent sigh of relief when Jared handed him a set of impossibly detailed notes that covered everything the worship arts pastor had just told him. *I'll just read these later,* Wes told himself.

Richard, the senior pastor, arrived about 10 minutes into the proceedings. He walked quickly across the stage to Jared, glancing at his watch on the way. Without so much as a greeting, he peppered the worship arts leader with questions: "Did the video changes get made? Can we see it after we're done here? Did you talk to your team about the color combinations? Last week's announcements went too long. Who's on this week?"

Jared nodded to Wes.

"Wes, you need to be quick, but not in a hurry," Richard instructed. "Measure your words."

Equal parts of exhilaration and fright washed over Wes. He was finally on the big stage, but he had no idea that everything about his participation in the services would be scrutinized so closely. How he stood, how many words he used, how he put his microphone on, and even what he wore—nothing was left to chance.

Or to personality, for that matter.

Wes canceled his scheduled time off on Friday and spent most of the day writing out and practicing his announcements and post-offertory prayer. The decision couldn't have gone over any worse with Jenny, though Wes tried to help her understand the weightiness of participating in the services for the first time.

Before the service on Sunday morning, Wes gripped his coffee cup tightly and tried to make small talk as he waited with the others in the cozy "green room." Richard brought everyone together for a "we're all on God's team" pep talk before leading the group in prayer. Just before the service started, Richard smiled at the group and offered four words of inspiration: "Feel free to succeed!"

Wes chuckled, but felt the words pass through him.

Afterward, as he sat in the services, Wes tried to justify the tension he'd been experiencing. *Excellence in ministry doesn't happen through good intentions, but through careful planning and execution,* he reminded himself. *The bar has been raised, and it's time for me to step up my leadership in the student ministry department.*

Unfortunately, that meant breaking the news to Jenny that his scheduled slowdown might not happen as soon as he'd thought. It occurred to him that his life was beginning to resemble his new home state. Unfortunately, it was more like California's traffic-ridden freeways than its scenic drives.

CHAPTER 4
START ME UP!

"I hate to interrupt such a nice conversation," Wes said as he checked his watch, "but I have a meeting at Starbucks."

"And you don't want to be late," Bonnie warned as she gave Wes a shove toward the door. "If you keep Melanie Rothschild waiting, we could all lose our jobs."

Wes headed for his midmorning coffee meeting with two moms, Michelle Evans and Melanie Rothschild. Michelle was one of the best and most delightful volunteers on the student staff. The high school girls in her small group adored her—as did the other student staff, who were frequently found at her house. The students called Michelle "Ripa" because her personality reminded them of Regis' talk show counterpart, Kelly Ripa.

Michelle had arranged the meeting so Wes could get to know her good friend and spa buddy, Melanie. Melanie was connected to seemingly every facet of life within a 10-mile radius of the church. Her husband was an elder and an investment banker who ran a fairly large hedge fund. They lived in a house that Michelle referred to as "the estate." Church and student events were often held there at the open invitation of the Rothschilds.

Melanie was involved in Junior League. She helped raise money for local schools. And she served as one of the teaching leaders of the Women's Bible Study ministry. Michelle referred to her as the "complete package." Melanie and her husband had two children: Clare, a smart, sweet eighth-grader; and Doug, a tall, chiseled high school junior. The Rothschilds were the quintessential Coastline family.

Wes and Melanie walked in the coffee shop together, but didn't realize they were meeting each other until they were both standing in front of Michelle. The three chatted briefly about their families and Coastline Church as they settled into their Barbie-sized booth.

"You know, Wes," Michelle said, "we're so glad you're here. The last eight months without a pastor have been difficult. Can you share with Melanie what you shared with us at the leaders' training meeting last week?"

Wes started slow, but his voice and tempo picked up as he hit some of his key thoughts.

"Reaching students works because more people come to faith during the teen years—especially during middle school—than any other time. Reaching students also might be the best and only way into the families in our community."

Melanie nodded and sipped her tea.

Wes continued.

"Sadly, most students have few significant adult relationships. So one of the areas that we're going to put time, energy, and resources into is our leadership. This is the—"

"You have no idea how good it is to hear you say that," Melanie interrupted him with a smile. "I can see your passion for this. I'm not nearly as involved as Michelle is, but I get a good picture of the youth ministry through my children. I think this is what the ministry has been missing, and you've come here just at the right time. I'm sorry—please continue."

Wes revealed his strategy for winning, equipping, and sending students. He shared his desire to raise the leadership bar high through a ministry team of students. He also talked in detail about his plan to expand the intern program so Coastline Church would be a place that served other churches by equipping and training youth pastors. Such a program would make the student ministry both deep and wide.

Melanie's response shocked even her good friend Ripa.

"I love that idea!" Melanie exclaimed. She then asked some quick and concise questions about the program Wes was proposing.

Thinking on his feet, Wes was able to give her some good answers.

"Okay, Wes," Melanie finally said. "I want you to do something for me. I want you to get me some numbers on what you think this intern program might cost over the next two to three years. Write it all up—costs, hurdles to overcome, everything. Then let's circle back and talk some more. Sound good?"

Wes repeated Melanie's request back to her to confirm the plan of action. *Sound good?* he thought. *Sounds great!* Melanie handed him her card as they walked out.

Michelle called Wes as soon as he got into his car.

"Looks like Jesus is doing something," she said. "If Melanie Rothschild wants this to happen, only he can stop it! You did such a good job of talking to her, Wes."

"So it might be Christmas for our ministry?" Wes asked with a laugh.

"You just sat on Santa's lap!" Michelle replied. "Now go write up your youth pastor Christmas list!"

Wes called Jenny at home and quickly filled her in on the morning's events as he headed to a lunch appointment at a little Mexican restaurant. When he walked in the place, a guy in his 40s stood up in the small lobby.

"You Wes?" the man asked.

"Yeah...Britt? How you doing?" Wes responded.

Wes had instructed Bonnie to set up this appointment a few weeks back, since he really wanted to get to know some other youth pastors in the area. Britt was the youth pastor at Trinity Presbyterian, a church large enough to have a youth pastor, but not much else students-wise.

Wes and Britt spent some time wading through the normal areas of affinity together. They talked about the local schools a bit as they ordered food and downed a basket of chips. Wes, still buzzing from his conversation with Melanie Rothschild, shared with Britt about his earlier meeting, his vision, and how close it was to coming together.

Britt congratulated him.

After several minutes Wes realized he'd done much of the talking and slammed on the brakes. He asked Britt about his ministry.

"How long have you been at Trinity?"

"Seven, going on eight, years," Britt answered.

"What do you like most about the ministry? What keeps you there?" Wes asked.

"Well, I guess it's many things," Britt explained between bites of his oversized burrito. "It's relational, you know—the church family, the staff, the students."

He paused.

"But it's also rhythm."

"What do you mean by *rhythm*?" Wes inquired.

"Well, I'm old and have worked on staff at a few churches. Some made it more challenging to actually practice what we preached."

"You mean ethically?" Wes interjected.

"Sort of," Britt replied. "But not in a strict moral sense. More along the lines of leading people to follow Jesus in ways that I wasn't always afforded the ability to."

Wes tried to connect to Britt's line of thinking by mentioning the frustrations of being a pastor, living in a fishbowl, and having the whole congregation as your boss.

Britt cut him off.

"Actually, that's not it at all."

Without further explanation, he launched back into his burrito.

"What could you not practice?" Wes asked after recovering for a moment.

"Healthy spiritual rhythm," Britt said. "I love ministry, but you know that can't define us as ministers. When it does it's easy for our ministry to replace our connection to Jesus, to our family, and to our friends. We give up our inner life rather than our outer life."

"So what happened? Did you blow out of ministry, get burned out?"

Wes was beginning to think he knew why Britt was at a small church after so many years in youth ministry.

"Actually it was the opposite," Britt explained. "The ministry was good by most of the standard measures. I guess I finally realized that many of those measures didn't work for me. Then I started dangerously wondering if they worked for anyone. I found it more and more difficult to minister at a place that asked people to rearrange their lives around following Jesus, but insisted on a ministry pace that didn't allow its pastors to do the same. I was out too many mornings, gone too many nights."

Wes was intrigued by Britt's explanation, but kept wondering what the real story was. Was it marriage problems? Or was it that Britt just wasn't cut out for a big church?

Wes glanced at his watch and saw it was time to go.

"If you need anything, let me know," he told Britt on his way out. "We do a few retreats and summer camp, and we're looking at going to a larger venue, so that might be real easy. It would be fun to do an outreach with a few churches together."

Britt thanked him and left the conversation open with "Let's talk more."

When Wes arrived home that evening, he told Jenny in detail about the day's meetings as they sat on the couch with the TV muted. His enthusiasm grew as he recounted the conversation with Michelle and Melanie. Jenny started to scribble notes. Wes smiled. He knew she would start outlining the proposal before he could ask. The potential before them was better than Red Bull for an energetic conversation.

"I also had an interesting lunch," Wes added, almost as an afterthought.

"How so?" Jenny asked.

"It was with the youth guy over at Trinity. Good guy, but older. I guess I wonder how you can be in a career for so long and not go anywhere. I don't mean for that to sound harsh. I'm just not cut out for that, with my skill set and gifts. It would drive me crazy! I have to be challenged."

"Isn't he motivated?" Jenny asked.

"I don't know. I think Britt might have had some bad experiences. Who knows? He might like being a big fish in a small bowl—or church, for that matter." He looked at Jenny and waved his arm for emphasis. "All I know is, if that's me in 15 years, please make me sell insurance or something. I don't want to be a youth pastor just because it's all I know how to do."

"I don't think we'll ever have that problem, dear," Jenny assured him.

What neither of them knew is how significant both Melanie and Britt would become in their lives—but not in the way they imagined.

Wes caught sight of Doug Rothschild as he was heading toward the door after youth group.

"Doug!" Wes called as he closed the distance between them.

"Whaddaya doing?" Wes said in his best New York accent.

"Nada, just heading home," Doug replied. "Tired."

"You got anything going this next week? Wondering if you'd want to hang, grab something at Chili's," Wes said.

"Yeah, I might be able to do that." Doug took his phone out of his pocket and thumbed through it for a second. "I think Thursday after practice might work."

"We could do dinner," Wes offered.

"I can always eat," Doug quipped back.

"I have something I want to run by you," Wes said with a hint of mystery in his voice.

"Uh...okay...there's some stuff I've wanted to talk to you about, too," Doug said.

"How about you text me when you're finishing up and are about to head over," Wes suggested.

"Okay. What's your number?"

Wes gave him his number, and Doug pinged him to make sure it was correct. They quietly stood next to each other for about a minute, entering information into their phones.

Doug finished and looked up.

"See ya."

"See ya Thursday, Doug," Wes replied.

Wes liked to say that Doug was "all upside." He was a great athlete who played both football and baseball. Given a free afternoon he could be found on the back nine of a nearby golf course. At 6'4" he was a dangerous combination of brains and brawn. Doug was the starting quarterback, though he was a junior. His relaxed attitude gave him a calmness that helped him perform well athletically, especially under pressure.

Doug's sway with other students was easy to see. Guys, girls, parents—everyone liked him—especially a loud group of sophomore girls from the church who formed the Facebook group "Doug Rothschild Is Proof That Heaven Will Be HOT!"

Doug was the perfect candidate for the ministry team Wes was forming. Wes planned to invite a number of sharp, spiritual, and influential students who could give grassroots ownership to the youth group. Wes believed if you give spiritual *alphas* the chance to lead, others will follow.

In Doug, Wes saw a young man with a strong and obvious leadership skill set. He wondered whether Doug was being challenged enough through the youth group's current programs. Wes wanted to give Doug a platform to use and develop his gifts.

Wes got Doug's text just before 6 p.m. on Thursday and headed for the restaurant. The two of them grabbed a table, ordered drinks, and talked sports as the flat screen across from them broadcast ESPN highlights.

Wes started into his ministry-team invitation just before their meals arrived. He told Doug about the vision he had for the youth group. He aimed his pitch right at Doug's competitive nature.

"I don't know of any youth group our size that's planned and run by students," Wes began, speaking slowly for emphasis. "We could be the first. If you're open to the idea, I want to give you and a few other students the leadership of the group."

And that's when the food came.

Without a word, Doug tore into his patty melt like he'd been holding a grudge against it. Wes made a show of taking a few bites of his cheeseburger, but between the carnage going on across the table and the butterflies in his stomach, he knew digestion was a lost cause. So he mostly stirred his iced tea, pretended to be interested in a rerun of the 2007 World Poker Tournament semifinals, and tried his best not to seem as vulnerable as he felt.

"The beautiful thing is that it won't take too much of your time," Wes continued after Doug polished off the last of his cheese fries. "We can talk and text during the week. I know you're busy with school and sports, but I do need honest engagement in your faith and the faith of other students."

Doug's response was slow and halting.

"I don't know," he said flatly. "I mean, it sounds cool and all, but I don't know if I'm the right guy. I don't feel very spiritual. I believe in God and everything, but lately I've had questions about God and how it all works."

"How *what* works?" Wes asked. "The team?"

Doug shifted uncomfortably in his seat.

"Well, I've been in church all my life. I became a Christian when I was six after church one day. I like it. It's a big part of my family and what we do. This last year after camp, I started trying to pray every night." Doug paused and glanced up at Wes. "But most nights I just feel like I'm talking to myself."

Wes seized the opportunity to counsel Doug. He assured the teenager his thoughts and feelings were normal. He talked about his own experiences with unanswered prayers and the times he felt like he was in a spiritual desert. He gave Doug some tips on praying and suggested he keep a journal to keep track of what God was doing in his life.

"The difficult thing with prayer is that feelings can fool us," Wes explained. "God is working, but often we just don't see it or experience it the way we want to. God hears us even when we don't feel like he does. I have dry times like that, too. I'm so impressed that you've been faithful."

Doug shrugged, but said nothing.

"It doesn't happen overnight. Let's keep talking about it," Wes offered encouragingly.

It's not just prayer! Doug wanted to shout. *It's everything! How can I lead other students when I can't get my own head straight? What am I gonna do, stand up there and say, "Thanks for sharing what God's doing in your life. By the way, it seems to me that you all see what you want to see. If something good happens, you give God credit. If something bad happens, you shield him from the blame." Oh yeah, I'd make a great spiritual leader.*

"Can we talk later about this prayer stuff and ministry team?" Wes asked as they got up to leave. "It could be that the ministry team will help the prayer stuff—steering a moving car, you know?"

Doug responded with a gesture somewhere between a nod and a shrug.

Wes smiled as he started his car. He couldn't wait to get home and share his good news with Jenny.

"Looks like the ministry is about to change!" he gleefully announced as he entered the door.

He had no idea how prophetic those words were.

It was Thursday morning when Wes' phone rang. He checked to see who it was and smiled as he answered.

"Ripa!"

Michelle's voice didn't ring out with its usual chipper tone. "Wes, what's going on with Doug Rothschild? Have you talked to him lately?"

"What, no greeting, Michelle?" Wes asked playfully.

"I just got off the phone with Melanie Rothschild, and it seems there's a little drama happening at the estate," Michelle said.

Wes' smile vanished.

"I guess last night Doug didn't go to youth group," Michelle explained. "He told his mom he was too busy and would rather not go anymore."

"You're kidding," Wes said as his face went blank.

"Anyway, the whole thing turned into a long conversation last night," Michelle continued. "I don't know much, but I do know she'll be calling. She's not one to take no for an answer, especially from her son."

Wes tried to recall his last conversation with Doug. It had been about two weeks since the two had talked at Chili's. They'd exchanged text messages since then, but Doug hadn't been to youth group. Wes thought he'd been busy with school and sports, but reality was setting in fast.

"What should we do?" Wes asked, trying to pull together a plan. "What did you tell Melanie?"

"I suggested she talk to you and Doug's small group leader, Dan. I told her you might have insight into what's going on with Doug."

"So did Doug say anything else?" Wes asked, hoping to uncover another piece of the puzzle.

"I don't know if it's a battle of wills or if something else is going on," Michelle said. "It didn't sound like he gave a lot of details to his mom and dad. I think—"

Traffic sounds drowned out the rest of her reply.

"What? Where are you?" Wes asked.

"I'm running into my yoga class," Michelle replied. "Always on to the next thing! I just wanted to give you a quick heads-up so you wouldn't be caught off guard if Melanie calls. You know how she is. She's a strong cup of coffee, but that's why I love her."

"Call me later if you get a chance," Wes said.

"Will do. Bye-bye, Wesley," Ripa replied. Only she could get away with calling him by his proper name.

Wes was finishing up lunch when the call came from Melanie. Their conversation was shorter and much more direct than Wes had anticipated. Melanie laid out the problems they were having with Doug, none of which was news to Wes. He made a few noises of agreement, but otherwise remained silent.

"Wes, where you can help is by meeting with Doug and talking with him, pursuing him," Melanie explained. "I think if you can close some ground, it would help. Doug has never been a problem, so I guess we had to have something happen sooner or later."

"Sure, I would love to get together with him," Wes said.

"Great, we'll take care of any expenses," she offered. Wes declined as the conversation came to an end.

Wes texted Doug after school and asked if he had any free time the following week. He didn't want to be too obvious and make the conversation more awkward than it might already be.

The phone rang, and Wes answered without looking at his caller ID.

"Wes, I heard you talked to Melanie Rothschild today."

It was Richard, the senior pastor.

"How did it go?"

Wes gave him the gist of their conversation, and Richard got down to business.

"I think it would be wise to try to meet with Doug as soon as possible," he said.

Wes agreed and told him they would be meeting the following Tuesday.

Richard became more blunt.

"What are you doing tomorrow?"

"It's my day off, but I guess I could meet with him," Wes said. He could already hear Jenny's complaints about his lack of days off.

"I think he'll be available after five," Richard continued. "Plan on picking him up at his house then."

That's when Wes finally understood what was happening: The Rothschilds had gone over his head. A wave of embarrassment and irritation washed over him. He'd never experienced anything like that before. *This is going to be awkward,* he said to himself. *Especially with my boss and the most powerful family in the church watching my every move.*

When he arrived at "the estate" the next day, the Rothschild family warmly greeted him and tried to make things seem casual and relaxed. But Wes still felt like he was on a blind date.

Wes and Doug drove to the Oasis, a place known for its menu of comfort food and tables and walls that had 30 years' worth of people's names carved into them. This time there would be no flat-screen TV to create a distraction. Wes and Doug settled into a booth that was almost completely enclosed.

"So what's up?" Wes asked. "We're both here for a reason."

"Sorry about that," Doug replied. "My mom—"

"Dude, no big deal," Wes interrupted. "This is just you and me talking. Does this have anything to do with our conversation at Chili's a few weeks ago?"

"Sort of," Doug replied in a low voice. "I guess I just feel like a hypocrite going to youth group. It's just not doing it for me...for where I'm at."

"Hypocrite?" Wes asked.

Doug began to share some of his doubts and questions. It was on topic with what he'd shared with Wes earlier—only much more scattered this time. His frustration was more evident, too.

Wes sensed that Doug was talking in circles, so he interjected.

"I'm sorry you're feeling this way. I don't know if it will help or not, but let me tell you what I see."

Wes proceeded to do what he did best: Make spiritual principles plain to a teen. He pulled out many of his best faith illustrations and analogies to give Doug some spiritual traction and help him move forward.

Doug sat quietly while Wes spoke. *You're saying the same thing everyone has been telling me,* he thought. *You're just using better examples. But it's all like some big tic-tac-toe game. It always ends the same.*

Wes took a break from his presentation, leaned back, and took a sip of his drink.

"Does that make sense?"

"I know what you're saying, Wes," Doug replied slowly. "I guess, like I told my parents, I just want a break from it all. I just want to not be frustrated by it anymore."

"Do you know what your parents are worried about?" Wes asked.

"That I'll walk away from the faith...and become a Democrat?" Doug said with a sarcastic sigh.

Wes wracked his brain for some other option, some way to get Doug to open up.

"Does this have anything to do with girls or something that happened with you in the past? I'm asking just in case."

"No, really nothing like that," Doug said. "Fortunately, there's nothing hidden in any closets."

"I didn't think so," Wes replied. "But I've had students confide to me that their relationship with Jesus became more difficult to understand when some things in their past came to the surface.

"You don't have to come to youth group to be involved," Wes explained. "It could be a few of us who meet to talk— or just you and me, if you want."

"Yeah, maybe." Doug's answer suggested he would most likely never take Wes up on the offer.

The ride back to the estate was quiet. Melanie greeted them as they came into the house.

"How did it go?" she asked.

"Good, we went to the 'O,'" Wes said. Doug nodded his head in agreement.

Wes knew that Melanie soon would find out the truth— the fact that nothing much had changed. He tried to speak some momentum into existence.

"We're going to see if we can get together more often."

Despite Wes' efforts, it would be months before he saw Doug again.

CHAPTER 7
DAZED AND CONFUSED

It was during a Tuesday morning staff meeting when Richard reviewed the numbers for the past month. Bonnie had pulled them for Wes, but he hadn't looked over them carefully. Richard caught something.

"Wes, I notice that numbers are slightly down this month. Anything going on?" he asked.

"Midterms this month, so our numbers are usually down a little bit," Wes explained.

"Did you look at last year's numbers?" Richard pressed.

"Um..." Wes said, as he flipped the page.

"They're off quite a bit," Richard pointed out.

Wes *hadn't* noticed. And now he was caught off guard in front of the other pastors.

He had nothing.

Trying to save face, he did some fast thinking on his feet.

"Well, we're trying to push more participation in our small group program for the next couple of months, so we won't lose momentum in the spring."

Wes almost believed it himself, it sounded so good. Shoot, it even felt strategic.

Richard clouded Wes' brief moment in the sun.

"Do you have numbers for the small groups?"

So much for strategy.

"No, sorry, I don't have them," Wes admitted. "Our leaders often don't get those to us. It's one of the tasks that fall to the end of the punch list."

"Get me the numbers you have," Richard said. "And if you're going to use small groups as a key measure, then make sure you have an accurate system in place."

Richard was off to the next item, but Wes could tell he wasn't exactly thrilled. It had been a number of months since Doug had stopped coming to the youth group. Richard's close relationship with the Rothschilds seemed to give the issue more mass. They had talked about the ministry, but Richard hadn't given Wes many compliments in those months.

Wes shot Bonnie an email about the small group numbers. When he got back to the office just before lunch, Bonnie handed him the small group numbers for the month.

"I don't think you're going to like them," she warned.

"You're kidding," Wes said as he scanned the page.

"We've been making calls for the last half hour, double-checking," Bonnie said. "When do you need to get them to Richard?"

"When they're good?" Wes replied.

"Maybe he'll look beyond the numbers," Bonnie said hopefully.

Wes cocked his head and fixed her with an "Are-you-completely-insane?" look. "This is a guy who, by his own admission, created statistically measurable goals for his marriage, his friendships, and his time with God," Wes reminded her. "I don't think it's in his internal wiring to look beyond numbers."

"So what's the plan?" Bonnie asked.

"I'll take them by Richard's office this afternoon," Wes said. "Then I think we're going to need everyone in tomorrow morning for a meeting."

Bonnie knew he wasn't joking when he headed to his office instead of lunch.

The next morning Wes pulled the youth staff together at 8:30 in the conference room. He'd delivered the small group numbers to Richard, but hadn't heard anything back yet. He wanted to have some precise insight into the attendance issue and a plan for addressing it before he met with the senior pastor again.

The staff offered several reasons Wes could empathize with for program attendance being down. But Wes knew Richard would not give ear to any of it. After 30 minutes or so, the caffeine started to kick in and disagreement broke out in the room. Wes smiled. He liked it when his staff got a bit punchy because he knew they were starting to think.

"Okay, we've wandered through the meadow of negativity," he said. "Let's talk about constructing something better. What can we do now to be proactive with leaders, students, and programs?"

Wes stood by the whiteboard with a pen in his mouth like a cigar, and the ideas started to flow. He jotted them down as quickly and succinctly as possible:

- *Revamp door prizes*
- *Leaders need to call kids*
- *More "Wow!" program moments*
- *We need to call kids*
- *Kids need to call kids*
- *Prayer room*
- *Blogosphere*
- *Text students before programs*
- *MySpace/Facebook groups*
- *Spend more time on campus*

"Okay, we've got some good ideas," Wes announced. "Now how do we tie them in with our strategy? What's still out of focus?"

One of the interns, Stew, said something that brought the meeting to a standstill.

"We could do a night like they do over at Trinity. Some of the junior and senior guys seem to like that."

"What guys?" Wes asked.

"Doug Rothschild, Ryan Ross, and Goodwin go there," Stew replied.

"What?" Wes asked. Stew started to explain what Trinity did on Sunday nights, but Wes cut him off. "Doug goes there? Don't Goodwin and Ross still go here?"

Stew nodded.

"Yeah, I think they do both ours and Trinity's some weeks."

"How do you know this?" Wes asked, though his real question was, *Why don't I know this?*

"Goodwin mentioned it at small group last week," Stew replied. "He said Doug made a deal with his parents. He'd attend services with his family and choose a Christian activity to be involved in twice a month."

"So how'd he get to Trinity?" one of the other leaders asked, saving Wes the trouble.

"Apparently his friend Darren was talking it up," Stew explained. "And I guess Doug liked what he heard."

"What do they do at Trinity?" Wes asked.

"Well, I've never been there," Stew said. "But I think it's like a debate—a town-hall conversation thing. They take a subject or Scripture passage and sort of talk around it."

"Like a small group Bible study?" Wes asked.

"It's cooler than that," Stew replied. "At least, that's how Goodwin describes it."

Wes wrote down "Town-hall Bible study" on the board and moved on. But he found he couldn't focus very well.

When the meeting was finished, he felt better about the numbers, but worse about Doug.

Is Doug really struggling with his faith—or just with our youth group? he wondered. *Maybe this is more my fault than I thought. And why didn't Richard tell me? I'm sure the Rothschilds told him. Why do I have to hear it from an intern?*

Wes pulled into the Starbucks lot a few minutes early for his meeting with Britt. As he waited for his fellow youth pastor to arrive, questions swirled through his mind. *Should I get right to the point and ask him what in the world happened with Doug? Or should I play it cool and let the subject come up naturally? What did Britt say to reach Doug? Or what did I say to drive him off?*

Wes took a deep breath and tried to gain his composure. Doug had walked away from his ministry. That felt like failure to Wes. Even worse, people close to the situation perceived it as failure, too. And as the folks at Coastline were fond of saying, "Gifted people in their gifted areas do not fail—they flourish."

Britt arrived, and they made small talk while they waited in line to order. When his turn came, Britt looked at the petite gal behind the counter.

"The usual," he quipped with a smile.

"Venti chi, no water," the gal behind the counter chanted to the barista.

Wes gave Britt a "Tell-me-that-didn't-just-happen" glance.

"What are you, a shareholder?" he asked.

"I should be," Britt answered. "I'm in here at least twice a day."

"How do you swing that?" Wes inquired. "My senior pastor would have my head—or count it against my vacation or something."

"No, I'm here doing ministry," Britt explained. "I meet students and leaders here constantly."

"Nice pull," Wes snickered. *No wonder he's at a smaller church,* he thought. "I just have too much in the pattern to hang out that much. Don't get me wrong, it would be nice."

"I guess it depends on what you feel is crucial to long-term spiritual growth," Britt answered. "I find earth tones and highly caffeinated conversation a must."

They grabbed a table and Wes weaseled around to the line of questioning he'd been sitting on.

"How's your ministry doing?"

"Good!" Britt said. "There are some pieces falling into place that have been a long time in the making." He started to explain some of the adult leadership issues he was facing.

"How's Doug doing?" Wes finally blurted. "I hear he's going pretty regularly to your group now. Is that helping?"

The question had just popped out of Wes, and he was a little embarrassed by the candor.

Britt thought for a second.

"He's good. Are you doing okay with that? I know Doug was a part of your ministry—"

Wes cut him off.

"That's cool, Britt. I'm really happy he's plugged in somewhere. I just think that my group is good for some students, and students who want something different might fit better in yours."

Britt deflected the arrogance in Wes' comment with a half smile.

"Knowing what you know about Doug, why do you think he feels comfortable with our group?" Britt asked.

"I don't know," Wes answered. "Could be your relationship. Could be that it's different from his parent's church. Could be a small-versus-large thing. Could be all of those things together."

"Actually, I don't think it is any of those things," Britt countered.

Wes was expecting Britt to agree with him. Though rattled, he attempted to appear calm.

"What do you think it is, Britt?"

"Doug told me a little bit about your conversations and what he felt," Britt said.

Wes immediately shifted into defensive mode.

"I met with him and talked to him," Wes explained. "He just never warmed up to me. To be honest, it's been a big deal to a number of people—including my senior pastor. So I do want to understand what's going on with Doug, for obvious reasons."

"Wes, your issue with Doug isn't church or youth group size or teenage angst or even parents," Britt explained. "It's about the importance of approach."

"Approach?" Wes asked.

"Yep, approach. Our goal as youth workers is to contextualize the Word of God, understand our audience— students and the world they live in—and help connect their story to God's story."

Wes felt a bit insulted.

"Are you saying I'm not doing that—or that I didn't do that with Doug?"

"Well, I guess I am," Britt replied. "But I truly think you just skipped some of the important steps."

"What steps?" Wes asked. "Like the Four Spiritual Laws?"

"No, the steps are a little more holistic than that."

"I don't know if I'm following you, Britt. What are you talking about?" Wes asked.

Britt looked directly into Wes' eyes.

"I've had too many students in my ministry walk away from Jesus," Britt admitted. "I felt good about their faith if they agreed with me and described their faith in terms that made us as a church feel good. Most of it worked for the short term, but not the long term. I'm talking about students who participated in Bible study, mission trips, and leadership teams. It didn't matter how involved they were. More than half of them walked away from their faith by the time they got to college. But I was unaware of it because everything in front of me was working, or seemed to be working. Students and parents were always happy with my ministry, leaders, and programs. But if my job was measured in the long term by how many students still had their faith intact three, five, or 10 years later? Well, I'd probably have been asked to leave!

"Too often I've set up a ministry program that would make the church, parents, and students happy for the short term, assuming that it would continue for the long term. But my experience is that this isn't true. I defined a student's faith by what made me feel good about them and hoped and prayed it would last."

"So that was the path Doug was on?" Wes asked.

"Honestly? Yes, I think it was," Britt answered.

Britt's frankness disarmed Wes.

"What did you do? What did you tell Doug?"

"I didn't tell him anything," Britt replied. "I just made sure he went through the steps. God did the rest."

"Okay, dude, what are these magical steps you keep talking about?" Wes said with a tense laugh. "You're starting to freak me out, cult boy."

"Wes, I'm messing with you a little," Britt admitted. "But I do want you to get the point. If we skip the important spiritual steps, we get to a results-driven faith that rarely lasts outside our context or youth group. So when kids go to college or transition into adulthood, they're not likely to bring their faith—at least, not that kind of faith—with them."

Wes nodded, but said nothing.

Britt continued.

"The question is: How do you teach them a *faith*, and not just a theology—a combination of biblical beliefs and real-life engagement? How do you remove yourself in the right way from the process? How do you help adolescents interact with God in the first person so they can build their own faith? That's what the steps are about."

Wes leaned in.

"Well, what are they, the steps? Fire away."

Britt leaned back.

"Do you really want to know? If you do them, it will change your ministry. And that's a dangerous thing."

What's the big deal? Wes scoffed to himself. *He's blowing smoke. Nothing could change my ministry that much. I've read most of the stuff out there on youth ministry. How different can his ideas be? Of course, if they worked for Doug, I should find out what they are. Then I can use the ones I like and ignore the ones I don't.*

"Are you sure?" Britt pressed.

"Bring it," Wes replied. "Bring your 'magic steps.' All kidding aside, I really would love to know what you've learned and how it helped Doug connect with God."

Britt wrote down some Scripture references on a piece of paper and handed it to Wes. "Here's some homework, so to speak. Read these passages so they're fresh in your mind when we talk again. What does your calendar look like?"

"Can we get together next week?" Wes asked. "I'm busy, but Wednesday mornings normally work."

"Sure, same time?"

"Sounds good."

Britt ended the conversation with a reminder.

"This is just between you and me, Wes. I'm being blunt with you because we're both youth workers who understand each other and the world we move in. I appreciate that trust."

Wes nodded and headed for his car. He had no idea that the next time they met, he'd be stretched to rethink his very approach to students.

Questions

CHAPTER 9
THE WIDER STORY

Wes was running late the following Wednesday. It was a busy week for him, but he didn't want to blow off his time with Britt. His calendar was packed, so rescheduling wasn't an option. It's no wonder Jenny had started referring to the youth group as Wes' "mistress."

"At least you know who my girlfriend is," Wes would joke.

When he'd told her about his meeting with Britt, she told him to ask Britt about life in a smaller fish bowl. Wes knew he needed to make some time for Jenny, and soon.

Britt was already seated when Wes walked over.

"Chi latte, no water?" he inquired.

Britt nodded.

"It's like being kissed gently by a unicorn that just slid down a rainbow."

"What are you talking about?" Wes asked.

"Sorry, I live in a house full of girls," Britt explained. "Order one and see if you're up to it. But I warn you, there's no going back."

"No going back?" Wes smirked.

"It's an enigma! You can try to devise an algorithm or use quantum physics, but nothing can explain the irresistible gravity that will continue to pull you to it again and again and again," Britt said.

Wes paused.

"You have no idea what you just said, do you?"

"Not really, but it works well on most of my students," Britt replied. "And they all fall prey to the irresistible gravity."

"Easy, Yoda, you don't have to use your Jedi mind tricks on me. I'll try one," Wes acquiesced.

On his way back to the table, Wes took a sip.

"Spicy...nice," he declared.

"Here come the chi physics," Britt warned. "Gravity is pulling your taste buds into the Starbucks' Death Star."

"Maybe you missed your true calling," Wes said.

They made small talk for a while until Britt turned the conversation.

"What did you think of the Scripture?" he inquired. "I know it's stuff you've read before."

"It was good," Wes said. "Was there a theme you wanted me to pick up on?"

"Yeah, there is," Britt replied. "But I wanted to talk over them in light of our ministry to students—and, more specifically, your ministry to Doug."

"What's the common denominator?" Wes asked. "Is one of the 'magic steps' secretly hidden in these verses, Pastor Da Vinci Code?"

"No, the steps are not 'magic' by any stretch of the imagination. They're essentially God's biblical example of building faith in people. I jokingly use the word 'magic' because it makes ministry to students engaging. To be honest, it was a very different approach for me at first because the ministry I used to toil and struggle over started to just fall into place."

"Did your time with Doug just 'fall into place'?" Wes asked.

"Well, yeah," Britt said. "It really did, in many ways."

"So what did you do?" Wes asked.

"Well, what did you see in the Genesis passage?" Britt asked.

"It's really all in there? Creation? The fall?" Wes wondered.

"No, look at the garden," Britt instructed. "How does God create man to live with him?"

"Well...in perfection, free of sin; in harmony," Wes answered.

"So why does God place the Tree of the Knowledge of Good and Evil in the middle of the garden?"

"So man has free will, a choice?" Wes answered.

"Yes, but think about it, Wes. Man isn't asking the question of God. God is instigating the question! He's pushing man to ask about his very nature, his very being. Is he a good God? Is he powerful and holy? Does his instruction work? God gives permission to question by placing that tree in the very center of the garden. The tree says even to a perfect man, 'You *can* ask and you *should* ask.'"

"But does that lead to the fall—or *a* fall?" Wes asked.

"Well, this is my very point." Britt sat upright in his seat. "Man falls not when he asks the question, but when he short-circuits the process."

Wes finished Britt's thought.

"Like when we act on the first advice given by the serpent." He thought for a moment. "So the first step is?" he said slowly.

"The original question," Britt replied. "Students have to be pushed to question the nature of...well, everything."

Wes thought for a second. "Couldn't that lead to students falling for the first advice they get? Doesn't it leave them vulnerable?"

"Absolutely, if that is all the further they go in the process," Britt explained. "But, truth be told, by not doing this instigative questioning, we leave them in an even more vulnerable position. We allow the real questions of life to be framed outside of faith. That means the questions are both asked and answered outside the community of faith."

Britt paused and looked up.

"I've been guilty of not doing this. What's that old quote? 'The church is in the business of asking only questions it has answers for.' No wonder so many of my students walked away from Jesus when they got to college or adulthood. The questions I never touched were finally asked."

"So you did this with Doug?" Wes asked.

"Well, that's my question for you," Britt said slyly. "Did *you* ask Doug any questions?"

"Yeah! Of course I did," Wes said a bit defensively.

"Did you really?"

"I think I did," Wes said. "Doug told me what he was thinking and feeling about his prayer life and his relationship with God."

"And?" Britt said.

"And..." Wes continued awkwardly, "I tried my best to answer his questions and engage him."

"Who did most of the talking?" Britt inquired.

"Well, I guess I did," Wes replied sheepishly.

"What percentage would you put on it, honestly?" Britt pressed. "Fifty percent? Sixty percent?"

"I'd say it was more like 75 percent," Wes admitted. "Maybe over 80 percent. In one of our last times together, Doug didn't say much."

"And you felt good about the answers?" Britt asked.

"Doug didn't, is that what you're saying?" Wes asked before blurting the obvious. "He never came back to continue the conversation. He went someplace else."

"The point is that an information dump isn't always the most effective way to help students connect with God. We often skip over the real questions instead of doing what Jesus did."

"What are the *real* questions?" Wes asked with a bit of cynicism in his voice.

"It depends on the person," Britt replied. "But tell me this: What were Doug's questions?"

"He said he felt like he was praying to himself when he prayed," Wes explained. "He didn't know if God was listening to him or if prayer really worked."

"So that's what you mainly talked about with him, prayer?" Britt asked.

"Well, yeah."

"Well," Britt said, "I don't think that was Doug's real question."

"So you're telling me Doug said his questions had to do with praying when they really didn't? You really do live in a house full of women," Wes said. "What are you suggesting, that we not believe what students tell us?"

"No," Britt quickly replied. "You have to listen and then be an instigator. How did Jesus use questions with the woman at the well in John 4?"

"He kind of teased her," Wes said.

Britt grabbed his Bible from his case and opened it up.

"He does sort of tease her by talking about 'living water.' But look at what he does when she asks for 'living water.'"

Wes' eyes moved along the page.

"He tells her to go call her husband."

Britt pointed to John 4:16.

"I know that statement is culturally loaded, but Jesus is being a total instigator with her," Britt explained. "And by doing so, some of the real questions about her life come to the surface. The brokenness that's been overshadowing her life is now open to discussion. Imagine how easy it would have been for Jesus to say, 'I am the living water,' when she finally asked for 'living water.' Instead, Jesus takes what seems to be a hard right turn into her personal life, a completely different direction."

Britt paused and looked up at Wes.

"So let me ask you again: What did you ask Doug?"

Wes thought for a moment.

"Well, I asked him questions—but mainly about prayer and his thinking. But you're right, I didn't really instigate beyond that. So what were Doug's questions and what did you end up asking him?"

"It's not a formula," Britt said firmly. "And it rarely happens in a meeting or two. With Doug, it took time for him to understand that I wasn't trying to fix him with verses, but wanted to help him figure out what was really bothering him. If a student can't question everything, then his faith can only be as wide as the questions allowed. This can lead him to a narrowing of his faith that can't engage much of life at all. No wonder many of my students left their faith as the questions in life got bigger."

Wes cringed at those words.

"Things *really* started to change when Doug started to ask the questions," Britt said emphatically.

"What kind of questions did he ask?" Wes asked.

"Well, those are Doug's to tell you. But I will say his questions were not about prayer. And he did ask, by far, the best questions I've ever had a student ask."

"So once you get him to ask the questions, you can figure out what the real issues are," Wes stated, believing he was finally on the same page as Britt.

"Not exactly," Britt said. "The original question is not a means to an end or a technique. It's the color, the flavor, and the ethos of everything you do with a student. I wasn't trying to outsmart Doug so he would listen to my answers. And I wasn't trying to get him to ask the questions so he would own the answers. My hope for Doug is that he will honestly approach God—and everything in life—knowing it's all on the table and open for discussion. I'm trying to help Doug hear from God directly and engage his life with God. This is what all the steps do. The first step is accomplished when students like Doug have the freedom God gave Adam in the garden, or the woman at the well. Isn't it interesting that Jesus, who *is* the Word, asks so many questions?"

"Well, what did you tell him?" Wes, a bit mystified, asked.

He wondered if he was really tracking with Britt.

"Truthfully," Britt said, "I didn't tell Doug anything."

"You didn't tell him anything?"

"Really, I didn't!" Britt insisted. "I just tried to be a spiritual instigator."

"What happened then? Doug opened right up?"

"Well, sort of," Britt explained. "Doug actually went right to step 2. Once he felt he had the freedom to question everything, the next domino automatically started to fall."

"And step 2 is?" Wes inquired.

"Step 2—" Britt began. "Step 2 will go against much of your thinking. But let's talk about that next time."

A wave of disappointment washed over Wes. He didn't realize how fast the time had gone by—or how much he wanted to hear what step 2 was.

"Next week work for you?" Britt asked.

"I think the same time will work. Let me check my Outlook," Wes said as he picked up his phone. "Same place?"

"Same place," Britt affirmed. "I'll email you some more Scripture for us to talk over next time."

As they left, Wes tried to figure out where Britt was going with this next step.

"How would it go against my thinking?" he whispered aloud. He already had much to process about his ministry and the questions he asked or even allowed. He knew deep down most of the communication he had with students was one-way. That's what he was good at, gifted at. What would the student ministry look like if the leaders in his group started to be instigators? Wes honestly didn't know if it would make things better or worse.

Over the next few days, Wes found himself paying more attention to his conversations with students. Maybe there was something to what Britt was saying.

On the other hand, Richard was still being Richard, and it seemed his interactions with Wes were getting shorter and shorter. Wes decided it probably wasn't the right time to bounce new ideas off him.

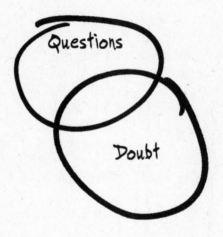

CHAPTER 10
THE END OF THE STORY?

It was an overcast morning in sunny California. Wes sat down across from Britt and launched into a complaint.

"What's the deal? I'm always cold here. The mornings are cold. The nights are cold. I thought this was the Golden State—as in brown, warm-toast golden."

"It's going to be sunny and in the mid-80s today. What're you complaining about?" Britt asked.

"Well it's not in the 80s or even the 70s right now. I never thought I'd need a sweatshirt and jacket in my car when I moved to California," Wes lamented.

"Maybe you could go back to the Midwest," Britt suggested. "I think it'll be warm there today. And humid!"

"Sorry, I take it back!" Wes said in mock desperation. "I repent. Just don't make me go back. I'm actually getting used to wearing hoodies."

"Now that we've solved your own personal global warming problems, want to continue our talk from last week?" Britt asked. "How are you feeling about our talk last week? Anything else come to mind?"

"Yeah, the more I think about it, the more I like it," Wes said. "But it does bring up more questions."

"So questions lead to more questions...interesting," Britt replied.

"No, I didn't mean that." Wes paused. "Actually, I sort of did. But if students are just asking questions, how do you get to the meat of Scripture? Is this just how you engage them after talks or in small groups?"

"Well, you could do a Sunday-morning series on questions or a whole year themed out on questions!" Britt said.

Wes caught himself before he answered in the affirmative. It took him a second to realize that Britt was being sarcastic.

"Sorry, the caffeine is kicking in. Was that a little strong?" Britt asked. "It sounds like you think questions are just a means to an end, a way to get kids into Bible study. Remember: Instigating questions is not a technique. Not that your small group leaders shouldn't instigate, but I think you're still thinking that our main task as youth workers is to give students God's answers. You're thinking that getting students into the meat of the Word is best accomplished by one-way communication."

Wes was trying to picture what his ministry would look like if he left students to figure out God's Word on their own. The image didn't sit right with him, and he knew it wouldn't sit right with his elder board and staff.

"What's bothering you about that thought?" Britt asked.

"It just doesn't seem like ministry to me—at least, not any ministry I've been involved with. It just sounds a little..."

Wes paused for a moment, trying to find a word that wouldn't offend Britt.

"Weak?" Britt offered.

"No, more touchy-feely," Wes replied.

"So you're thinking Chuck Norris and I'm describing Richard Simmons?"

Wes laughed. "Okay, I guess I'm thinking that ministry should feel like laser tanks driven by Batman, followed by ninjas with light saber nunchucks. But I don't know how that would work."

"Wow!" Britt exclaimed. "You are a youth pastor! I don't want to know what other scenarios are dancing around in your head."

"Dude, *you* brought Richard Simmons into the conversation!" Wes bantered back. "Honestly, they hired me at Coastline to lead, speak, and plan. And this step seems a bit out of pace with that. I mean, we ask students questions all the time, but they're normally follow-up questions in our small groups."

"Let me ask you this," Britt said. "Did Jesus instigate questions that were stretching for the disciples? Or did he ask questions so the disciples would all be on the same page?"

Knowing a rhetorical question when he heard one, Wes said nothing.

"Do you have uniforms, too? Do you feel better when your kids all wear the same youth group shirt?" Britt was really trying to make his point stick, so subtlety was out the window. "What makes a good youth group doesn't always make a good disciple. So which one are we after?"

"I see your point," Wes said. "I'm just having trouble connecting the why with the how. How would that ministry look? Where would we be taking students?"

"Let's forget about being pragmatic for a moment," Britt suggested. "Don't think about your youth group programming now. The steps are not a programmatic approach. I think of them as almost the opposite of a program-driven ministry. But that's a different conversation. The steps are the flavor of your ministry. But the point you've hit on is crucial. Where *are* we going with students? And, no, it's not to make them like Richard Simmons or Chuck Norris. Don't oversimplify the first step. It's just the starting point."

"So what's the next magic step?" Wes asked. "I'm clueless."

"What did you think of the verses this week?" Britt asked.

Wes hadn't really looked at the verses that closely. In fact, he'd just glanced at them. Thanks to seminary, he was able to recall just enough information about a Scripture passage to make it difficult to see it in a new light.

Britt continued.

"I want to talk about Thomas. What do you think of his story?"

"I like the fact that Thomas is redeemed by Jesus even though he doubted," Wes contributed.

"Really?" Britt smiled. "Do you see any part of yourself in Thomas?"

"Yeah, of course," Wes replied. "I feel like Jesus comes after me when I make mistakes. And God tells me I'm still his and still useful."

"What part of Thomas' story are you thinking of?" Britt asked.

"I'm thinking of Thomas' doubt of Jesus' resurrection and the picture of Jesus coming to him, showing him his scars," Wes said. "I don't doubt God like *that*, but sometimes the way I live, the decisions I make, I feel like I practically doubt him."

"That's encouraging to hear," Britt said. "I think doubt is a good thing."

"A good thing?" Wes asked, a bit perplexed. "That's not what I meant."

"Yeah, a good thing—a needed thing. Doubt is a good thing. What you said was really transparent."

"Dude, how is doubt a good thing?" Wes asked.

"Spiritual doubt is necessary for us to move forward in our relationship with God. By the way, it's also the second step," Britt explained.

Wes' mind started to reel as he wrestled with the idea of doubt being a good thing in his ministry. Wasn't doubt what caused students to struggle and walk away from their faith? He voiced his concerns to Britt.

"What's the opposite of doubt?" Britt asked.

"Faith?" Wes answered, unsure.

"Maybe that's the reason you're having a difficult time with this step," Britt explained. "If you think of doubt as the negative side of faith—the faith killer—then how can that ever be good?"

"Well, what *is* doubt then?" Wes asked.

"Glad you asked." Britt's energy level cranked up a notch. "What if doubt is like the end of a bad story? In order for the story to continue, there has to be movement. You know the difference between a great movie sequel you can't wait to see and...*Breakin' 2: Electric Boogaloo?*"

"What?" Wes chuckled.

"Sorry, dude, I'm from the '80s," Britt explained. "Anyway, I think honestly spoken doubt helps our faith story continue and transition to something better. Without it, the story ends—or becomes trite and boring. Faith is paradoxical in that, for it to continue, we have to constantly doubt our wrong thoughts and beliefs about God. When we do, the story of God can continue and get bigger, better, and richer. Have you ever doubted God, Wes?"

Wes didn't know how to answer. If he doubted God, what did that say about his leadership?

Britt continued.

"If we don't allow doubt to come to the surface, the story is likely to stagnate—or, even worse, end. Make no mistake: Sooner or later, doubt *will* come to the surface in students' lives. After all, it's their place in life to rethink everything. I can completely get why doubt, in the context of faith, seems like a bad thing. We've both seen students' stories with God end. When they experience doubt, they often feel as if they have only two choices. The first is to spiritualize the doubt, to try harder and tell themselves that their story is good and working—even though it's not. The second option is for them to walk away from their faith and allow their story to end while they pursue what seems like a better story."

Britt paused.

"So I like the third option!" he said. "Using doubt to propel students into God's story. If we don't, someone else may propel them into a different story."

"So how do you do that without it being hurtful or causing students to leave the church?" Wes asked. "My church hired me to do the contrary, you know?"

Wes had the feeling that if Richard overheard this conversation, he'd be fired tomorrow.

"When students doubt, they're actually owning their faith," Britt explained. "When they start to question and rethink what's been told to them—I believe it's a sign of ownership and individualization. They're trying to make faith tangible in their hearts and minds. If they're going to stand before God alone, they have to own their faith. They can't use their parents' faith or their friends' faith. That feels terrifying as a pastor. But I think it's a crucial step in their developmental journey as they integrate their new body, brains, and emotions on the path to full adulthood. Faith must be integrated, too, and doubt is a healthy expression of that."

Wes stared at Britt. There were so many different things he wanted to say, but he couldn't verbalize any of them.

"Let's go back to the Thomas verses," Britt suggested. "Is he really 'Doubting Thomas'?"

"Well, he did doubt, and his name was Thomas," Wes replied.

"Besides that. See, I think Thomas was brutally honest. He didn't doubt Jesus' life and ministry, but he couldn't fathom the resurrection. Maybe he was extraordinarily scientific and needed hard evidence. I've totally had students like that in my group. Maybe Thomas was very emotional and didn't want to believe that Jesus was back because his heart was broken. Regardless, what does Jesus do for him?"

"He told him he could stop doubting and believe," Wes answered.

"Look what Jesus does!" Britt exclaimed. "He gives Thomas what he needed to believe, to allow Thomas' story to continue. I don't think Jesus was scolding or shaming Thomas by showing him his scars. I think Jesus understood what Thomas' doubts were and what he needed. It's interesting that Thomas couldn't be convinced by the other disciples' answers, but he was still with them. What does that tell us about the community they had and the part it plays in giving permission for people—even disciples—to follow at different speeds?"

Britt paused to make sure Wes' head wasn't going to explode.

"I'm obviously using doubt in the most positive of terms," he continued. "The word *doubt* covers a lot of ground, like the word *love* or *eBay*. I think with students it's more like the words spoken to Jesus in Mark 9: 'I believe, help my unbelief.' You know? 'You will seek me and find me when you seek me with all your heart.' Naming doubt is about building faith. We have to do both. Moving in and out of doubt is part of the process. So, where do students go to express their doubts?"

"Most likely to each other, their parents, and sometimes, if we're lucky, us," Wes said.

"I think you're absolutely right!" Britt said. "But why friends?"

"Other students are safer," Wes thought aloud. "They listen and obviously identify with each other. We, on the other hand, often have agendas for them."

"Have you ever asked any of your students this?" Britt inquired.

"Asked them what?"

"Asked them who they share their doubts with?" Britt explained. "Try it and see what you get. I'd be interested to know what they say. But what if..."

Britt paused for a second.

"What if doubt is the new black? What if students who honestly doubted were the ones searching after God?"

"It would give a whole different meaning to being a fully devoted follower," Wes said with a chuckle.

"Like Jesus did when he chose fishermen and tax collectors?" Britt asked.

"Yeah, maybe like that," Wes said. "I don't know. I have to think about it some more." Out of habit, he started thinking of ways he could organize this information, program it, and teach it to his staff.

"Remember, it's not a formula or program," Britt reminded him after studying the intent expression on his face. "It's a holistic approach to doing ministry."

Wes nodded.

"Good, then our work here's done for today," Britt said, pushing his chair back.

"You know, you're different than I thought you'd be," Wes confessed to Britt as they walked to the parking lot.

"Is that good?" Britt asked.

"Yeah, it's good," Wes assured him.

"Thanks. I hope you still feel that way about me next time."

"What's the next step?" Wes asked with a smile. "Oh, wait, maybe we should wait awhile so I can digest what we've been over."

"Wow!" Britt said. "How did you know?"

"Know? What do I know?" Wes asked. "Another Jedi mind trick? Speaking things into existence? Well played!"

Wes had hit on the next step without even knowing it. He wondered what his staff would say if he told them he wanted them to get their students to doubt. He already knew how Melanie Rothschild felt about it. He definitely needed time to sort through all of it before presenting it to anyone. The last thing he needed right now was to appear to not have it together. It seemed ironic that, only a few months earlier, he'd felt so sure of himself and his ministry. Maybe Britt was right. Maybe this would change everything.

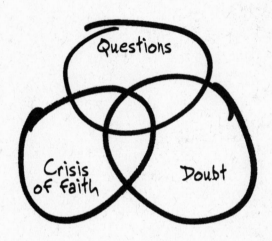

CHAPTER 11
THE BUILDING STORY

Wes was already waiting at the cafe when Britt entered and took his place in line. Wes jumped up and joined him.

"I almost ordered for you, but I couldn't bring myself to order...tea," Wes said with mock disgust.

"Dude," Britt shot back, "all the cool kids drink tea!"

"I'm a coffee guy. I just can't do it," Wes explained.

"Maybe that's the problem," Britt stated bluntly.

Wes chuckled until he saw the solemn look on Britt's face and realized Britt wasn't joking.

"So if I drink tea, I'll be cool," Wes said. "Is that the next step—be cooler than students?"

"I think that's technically what youth ministry used to strive for," Britt replied. "But the coffee-tea dilemma might be a good illustration of what we're going to talk about."

"Did you like the chi you had a few weeks ago?" Britt asked.

"Yeah, it was good," Wes acknowledged. "I'm not just saying that, either. It had a unique flavor to it."

"So why wouldn't you order it again?"

"Well...I guess I just like coffee and don't see myself as a tea drinker," Wes explained.

"So it's the taste?"

"Not entirely," Wes said. "Chi is actually more...*tasteful*. Is that a word? I'm just used to coffee. I might drink chi once in a while, though."

"So how do you change?" Britt asked. "How do you personally come to a place where you're open to becoming a tea drinker and forsaking your coffee-drinking ways?"

"Well, I don't know." Wes paused to think. "I guess I'd have to like tea much more than coffee. Again, I might have a chi here or there. It just wouldn't be my drink of choice."

"I know this might seem like a silly point to talk about. Who cares what we like to drink? Personal preference, right?" Britt said. "I guess I'm interested in the why behind that personal preference. I can't make you like my chi tea latte, can I?"

"Not really," Wes said.

"Well..." Britt hesitated, trying not to sound glib. "isn't that what we tend to do as youth workers? Try to talk students into preferring Jesus in parts of their lives when they have little motivation to do so? I wonder if that's one of the reasons many students don't carry their faith forward in life."

"So we don't tell them about Jesus? I mean, isn't there a big difference between what you believe and base your life on, versus what grande, half-caff, overpriced drink you prefer on any random morning you show up here?"

Wes' frustration boiled over as he tried to make sense of where the conversation was heading. He'd spent the whole week wrestling with their last conversation only to find himself engaging in this bizarre comparison.

"No, I'm not saying that at all," Britt countered. "I'm just wondering: If our goal is to make coffee drinkers into tea drinkers, what are our methods for doing so? Just because they drink tea in front of us and seem to enjoy it, does that make them tea drinkers for life? Did it work on you when you tried the chi awesomeness?"

Britt paused.

"I guess I'm interested in the bigger question of how people change for good," he stated.

Wes started to respond, but Britt interrupted and continued his thought.

"What would it take for me to make you a tea drinker today?"

"Irrefutable proof that tea will make me live 100 more years and make me sexy—like Matt Damon, *Bourne Identity* sexy!" Wes said. "Or proof that coffee will give me cancer and back hair, lead to bankruptcy, and fill me with a deep desire to watch Richard Simmons workout videos!"

"So you want me to scare you into it?" Britt asked.

"Yep! Absolutely," Wes said. "Convince me. Scare me. Do what you have to do!"

"Doesn't work," Britt told him. "Wish it did, but it doesn't for most people."

"Sure it would, if those things were true," Wes argued.

"Well, the state of our current health-care crisis seems to argue against that," Britt countered. "My physician friend Ramesh summed it up to me this way: Much of our current health crisis is based on behavior that can be changed, like overeating, drinking, smoking, lack of exercise, and good old-fashioned stress. Trying to reason with or scare people with the truth of their life preferences has little long-term effect on most people. In other words: Many of our health-care problems are due to behaviors that could be changed, but aren't—to the point people actually die rather than make the changes! My point is that it's not easy to change, even when the need for change is obvious."

"That may be true," Wes conceded. "But I wouldn't keep drinking coffee if it was like..."

"Cigarettes?" Britt finished his thought.

"Yeah."

"Have you ever talked to someone who tried to quit smoking?" Britt asked. "Many of them tell a different story."

"So change has to be dramatic or big?" Wes asked.

"I think, for long-term change, a better story will last longer than fear or statistics," Britt reasoned. "For example: A friend of mine tried and tried to lose weight. The idea of eating healthy food that she didn't like made her feel like she was striving to live a longer, but more miserable, life. Seeing her grandchildren, on the other hand, gave her a better story and new motivation to lose weight. She needed a bigger story, no pun intended."

"So, if I read you here, we need to give students a bigger story to help them change?" Wes asked. "Isn't that exactly what we're trying to do?"

"Absolutely," Britt agreed, "but we should do it as spiritual catalysts rather than information givers."

"So what does that look like in your ministry?"

"Well, actually," Britt said, catching Wes' eyes, "we have to be able to do something that might seem dangerous."

Wes sat up and leaned in. *Dangerous* always sounded cutting edge, and he liked cutting edge.

"We need to give students the freedom to have a crisis of faith," Britt explained.

Wes' youth pastor brain was already struggling with the concept of doubt being positive. The thought of allowing a crisis to happen sounded like an especially bad idea. He could picture the look on Richard's face when he told him their students needed crisis.

"No offense, Britt, but I think my church hired me to do the opposite," Wes said.

"Well, what do you think crisis in a student's faith looks like?" Britt asked.

Wes thought about Doug.

"Well, it might look like someone with no way forward, someone who wants to give up or give in."

"What if it's tension, spiritual tension?" Britt asked. "Every good story has tension, and tension is what makes the story good. Without it, how much change can occur?"

"That's not been my experience," Wes countered. "Usually if a student has doubt or crisis, they drop out sooner or later."

"Why?" Britt asked.

Wes was starting to understand Britt's thinking.

"The story ends," he said. "But what if they don't care if the story continues?"

"That's been my experience also," Britt agreed. "Students who aren't allowed to embrace tension are very likely to just walk away. I completely agree with you. Every time I've tried to talk a student out of a place of tension or have him skip over it, he most often drops the story."

"So how does this tension work?" Wes asked.

"I think God's design is to give us space to work things out. This is especially true for adolescents in how they process all of life, not just their faith. Let's look at the journey of people who continued to discover God. Saul is blinded on the road to Damascus, and what happens?"

Wes filled in the blank.

"He sits and waits."

"It's interesting to see how many people wait on God to discover him anew."

"When you say it that way, I get where you're going," Wes said.

"Is it easier to identify with this step if I wrap it in Christian-speak?" Britt asked rhetorically. "I think so. But I purposely use the word *crisis* because there's nothing easy about it. The process pushes us beyond our comfort zone to a place where we're forced to deal with God on his terms. Again, a student's story continues and becomes a better story, though not necessarily a better life. That might seem counterintuitive to us as Americans, the idea that our stories get better when there's struggle. I just believe spiritual tension brings our relationship with God into the spotlight."

"So where in Scripture do you take this from?" Wes asked.

"You tell me," Britt fired back.

The answers came to Wes like waves rolling onto a shore.

"David, Abraham, Peter, Moses," he said. Maybe Britt was on to something.

"Did any of them have a clear and perfect relationship with God?" Britt asked.

"No, you're right," Wes acknowledged. "Their stories are about them discovering God in the worst situations."

"Tension defines their faith," Britt added. "The book of Psalms is packed with tension and the raw interaction it created. You've got David crying out, brokenhearted, in deep wonder. With all he saw the Lord do, he still experienced significant tension. So maybe being a man after God's heart means having permission to wonder and wait. What if that tension was the mark of a disciple? Who would be the disciples in your youth group?"

They both sat quietly for a moment, thinking about the question.

Britt continued.

"Don't you think Jesus' disciples were at their best when they experienced tension? Think of how Jesus led them to experiences that caused them to reframe their thinking about their theology and culture. Think of Peter out of the boat. Think of Jesus touching lepers, scolding the religious leaders, befriending prostitutes, and clearing out the temple. All of that created tension."

Wes nodded.

"Did the disciples recognize the value of that tension immediately?" Britt asked.

"No, it was some time later," Wes answered. "But what if this doubt-and-tension approach works for a few students but drives others away?"

"If it's a method, or the next new program or technique, then you'd be right," Britt acknowledged. "There's nothing plug-and-play about this. It's based on sincere relationships, knowing enough about a student's story to connect it to God's story. It could be disastrous if it was used to manipulate people."

"I understand what you're saying, but I don't know if I'm sold on the concept yet," Wes admitted.

"Need more time to work it out?"

The lights came on and Wes started to laugh. "Dude, none of your Jedi mind tricks."

"Ironic, huh?" Britt said with a smile.

Wes hadn't realized he'd been experiencing the very steps they'd been talking about. When he did, the realization struck him like the end of a good movie. How had he not seen it happening?

"So what's next?" he asked with a chuckle. "Are you going to go all David Blaine on me and ask, 'Is this your card?'"

"No, no card tricks or levitation," Britt replied. "I hope you realize that this is the same process I go through all the time. I think it's how we grow. But next time, let's do something different. Can we meet for breakfast a week from Saturday down at Pipes, right off Highway 1?"

Wes checked his schedule and agreed—but with a condition. He asked to meet a little earlier so his morning wouldn't be completely taken from Jenny.

Wes was still conflicted as he headed back to the office. He had no idea what the next step was, but smiled because he figured the new location and time had to be part of the plot. Wes was starting to understand Britt and how intentional he was. Wes' instincts were spot-on. Britt did have a plan for the last step. What Wes didn't guess was that Britt wouldn't actually talk about the final step that next Saturday.

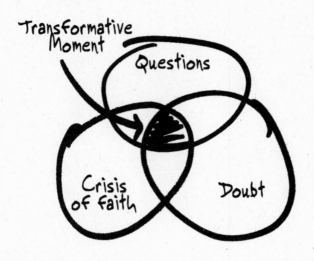

CHAPTER 12
THE BETTER STORY

Wes drove by the restaurant looking for parking. *Why did we meet all the way over here?* he wondered. Pipes was more of a shack than a restaurant—a block or two off the beach, and most of the seating was outside. He threw on a sweatshirt as he stood on the sidewalk and scanned the tables for Britt.

To his surprise, he spied Doug at a table.

Britt was sitting next to him.

"Stinkin' Jedi!" Wes muttered with a sheepish smile, his pulse quickening.

Britt and Doug both stood up to greet him. That's when Wes realized why they were meeting down by the beach. The wet, scraggly hair gave them away. They'd been out surfing that morning.

"You guys go out?" Wes asked, kicking himself for the high concentration of stupidity in the question.

"Yeah, I went out," Britt said. "I didn't come in very well, but I went out. Doug here's the guy."

"No," Doug said, shaking his head. "It's the only thing I like to get up early to do. And this is a nice break. Normally it's too crowded."

They ordered breakfast and talked for a while. Wes was reserved and carefully chose his words with Doug. He'd never felt this awkward with a student before. But in light of his past conversations with Britt, he found himself second-guessing everything he said. He didn't want to screw this up—not because of what Richard would think, or Melanie—but because over the past few weeks, he'd started to rethink a lot of stuff.

Britt allowed the banter to continue until they were in the middle of their oversized breakfast burritos.

"Wes," Britt said between mouthfuls, "we've talked a lot about ministry over the past month or so. I know Doug was a big part of that for you. So I thought it would be fitting for him to share about the last step."

Wes had no idea where this would go. He sensed he'd be apologizing to Doug at the end of the morning. His mind drifted back to the conversations they'd had.

Doug spoke up.

"I really wanted to talk to you. So when Britt asked me about coming this morning, I was all in," Doug told Wes.

Britt turned to Doug.

"Over the last month Wes and I have been getting together to talk over youth pastor stuff," Britt said. "Much of it has centered on how students own their faith—you, for example. In other words, what happened to you when you came to Trinity."

There it was. But Britt wasn't finished.

"Specifically, what we've been talking about is the steps students need to take to help them own their faith," Britt said.

This wasn't new information to anyone. Wes and Doug had both walked through the steps. But Britt knew that going over it would help the conversation.

"The first step we talked about was questioning. Students only frame their faith as wide as the questions they ask and really wrestle with. This leads naturally to the second step, spiritual doubt. The idea behind this step is that doubt is a catalyst for owning one's faith and allowing the faith story to continue. When a student is able to question and then doubt, the third step comes to the surface—crisis of faith. This idea is that deep change with God happens when students experience spiritual tension and are given space to work things out."

Wes was a little surprised Britt would share his ministry approach with Doug.

"So what's the next step in your grand plan?" Wes asked, hoping it would be simple but knowing nothing had been easy up to this point.

"I thought I'd have Doug tell you," Britt said as he took a drink and sat back.

Wes didn't know how to feel about that. He wanted to hear what Doug had to say but felt as if it might be belittling to Doug to say it out loud.

Doug started in.

"First, I want to thank you, Wes. You really helped me, and leaving Coastline was not about you," Doug said.

A wave of relief washed over Wes. He found himself wishing Richard were around to hear Doug's words and wondering if Melanie knew. Wes hated that those thoughts came so quickly and naturally these days. He realized he was completely enmeshed in the Coastline Church culture and its narrow definition of wins and losses.

"Your talks got me thinking," Doug continued. "You shared that you struggled at one time and that sort of stuck with me. But let me back up. When you came, I'd been struggling with some thoughts for a while."

"The idea that your conversation with God felt distant at times?" Wes asked.

"Yeah, that was part of it," Doug said. "But it wasn't just the prayer thing. I didn't quite know what it was. My faith just wasn't working the way everyone else said it should. When you and I talked, you said many of the same things to me my parents said. The answers weren't bad, but they also weren't where I was at. I don't know if you got that vibe, but every time I talked about it, it would just frustrate me."

"So let me understand this," Wes said. "Britt, who frustrates me, somehow un-frustrated you?"

They all laughed.

"Okay, I know where your frustration went. He's not a pastor, he just transplants frustration!"

"That's funny," Doug said, "because one time he was asking me these questions and I was trying to figure out if he was helping me or trying to confuse me. My friend Darren calls him Pastor Psych because he's always in your head. Anyway, for the record, I didn't go over to the youth group at Trinity. The youth group sort of came to me."

"How so?" Wes inquired.

"A few late-night conversations with my friend Darren and his friends, who did some of those things Britt described in the steps. We started talking about our faith one night, and they kind of just put it out there."

"What do you mean?" Wes asked.

"Like one night these girls started talking about what heaven would be like. They said things that were better than any sermon I've heard. What would heaven look like and be like? How would Jesus appear and look and feel to us? What would relationships be like? One girl was convinced

Jesus would still have a body because he had one after the resurrection and she wanted a hug."

Doug laughed as he continued.

"And her friend Audrey kept saying it would be stupid because for all eternity people would be lined up to talk to Jesus. Like one big attraction at Disneyland. Heaven would basically be a big crowd around Jesus trying to get his attention. We talked about it until like two in the morning. Anyway, I just needed that sort of open questioning. It was the first time in a while my faith had energy."

Wes was glad to hear of Doug's energized faith, but he couldn't help compare youth groups. He'd always thought of the Coastline youth group as the largest and most dynamic in the area. That thought quietly fed his ego. Hearing Doug talk made him question what ripple effect the students in his group were really having. What conversations were happening outside of the church? A layer of Wes' confidence eroded.

Doug continued.

"When I met Britt and another leader, Bob, I started to understand why Darren and his friends related to God the way they did. Britt and I talked a number of times, and he did that whole question, doubt, step thing. He was completely honest. I felt like he really wanted to know where I was at. I think he also wanted me to know what was bothering me, something I'd not been able to put my finger on."

"I'm sorry you didn't feel that in our conversations together," Wes said a little sullenly.

"No, Wes, you've always been very honest. And I think you tried to solve my problem. I just didn't need you to solve my problem. Dude, that last time we talked? You have to know I told my mom to apologize to you for that. I felt so bad."

"I felt like I was a blind date, going to prom!" Wes admitted. "I should have brought a corsage."

He and Doug laughed and then filled in Britt on the back story.

"So what made the difference?" Wes asked.

"Well, the tension step was obvious," Doug explained. "But instead of pushing me to believe or accept an answer, Bob said something that just made sense to me. He said it might take time to understand some of the faith questions we were talking about. He was saying it to a few of us at the time, but it really hit me. He said it was after college some of this stuff finally made sense to him. He said, 'I'd been asking questions I couldn't understand the answers to yet. The longer we think about it the better it gets.' Britt told me a number of times that frustration is change about to happen. It forces us to connect the dots. That helped me stop worrying and made me start to feel that something good, rather than bad, was happening to me."

"That's great. So you feel better about your faith and your questions and connecting to God?" Wes asked. He really was excited Doug had found what he was looking for, even though he'd needed to go elsewhere to find it.

"The issue wasn't just with my prayer life, as I told you," Doug said. "It was actually bigger than that. I wondered: If I'd grown up in a different family, would I believe differently? Is my faith *my* faith, or just what my parents want me to believe? If I were born in China or India, what would I believe? I think when the questions got bigger, it helped me start to understand my family and faith better."

"That's good...um...that's what I was trying to say," Wes joked. "So where are you now?"

"Right here," Doug said. "But that's not the best part. When my questions were bigger, I started asking God *better* questions. Well, better questions for me. One night as I was reading through the book of Matthew and journaling, I had this overwhelming thought: That God's love for me would be the same no matter where or when I was born. Jesus came here for everyone. I know that might seem simple, but it wasn't just a thought. It was like God whispered in my ear that night. It was something I thought, felt, and understood. And it hit me in my soul. Does that make sense? It was like part of the frustration you saw before disappeared. It was just really cool!"

"That's the last step," Britt chirped on cue, "a transformative moment. A moment that's directed by God's Spirit when a student's story and God's story come together. Jesus, speaking in the first person into a student's story, quiets the crisis, relieves tension, and brings peace."

"Yeah, it's not that I got just an answer," Doug said. "It's that God's bigger story seemed to cover it. I think peace is a good word. I kept looking for an answer like some sort of mathematical equation that just never added up for me. I think that's why my talks with you or my parents usually ended in frustration. It turned out I needed God himself to be my answer."

"That's sweet action," Wes declared. "Did Britt tell you to say all that stuff? Did he give you a script?"

Wes couldn't help but smile widely. Doug wasn't a casualty of lost faith. Wes forgot about the church politics and his personal issues and was simply happy.

"You know," Britt said, "one of the things that's been pressed into me over my 20-some years of ministry is that I have to get out of the way. I'm a guide who directs students into the presence of God. The difficulty is I'm so excited about who God is that I want to do it all. I overstep. I'm not the mediator between God and man, Jesus is! But for years in my youth ministry, I felt like I was the mediator. The youth group needed me in order to become close to God. Anyway, the steps are an attempt to create an environment where students connect directly to Jesus. They hear from him."

"Hey," Wes exclaimed, "you said it wasn't a program! Remember? 'The steps are not a program'?"

"Program shmogram!" Britt barked. "They aren't, young Wesley. They're the environment, the culture, the vibe we're trying to create. I think when you create that, and create it well, most *any* program will work."

They talked for a while more, and Wes lost track of time. The call from Jenny brought him out of his cocoon.

"I'm just leaving and heading home," Wes told her. He couldn't wait to talk to Jenny about his conversation with Doug and about Britt's last step. He knew by the tone in her voice he'd better take her someplace nice to talk.

"Doug, you made my week. Thanks for the morning, guys. I have to bolt!" Wes said as he stood up.

"Obi Wan Kenobi, next week?" he asked, looking at Britt.

"Sure, shoot me your schedule," Britt replied.

CHAPTER 13
WALK THIS WAY

"What are you mumbling about in there?" Jenny asked as Wes crammed his small suitcase full of clothes. He was on his knees, taking extra time to fold his shirts carefully so they wouldn't be wrinkled.

"Why are you taking those shirts to the middle school retreat this weekend?" Jenny asked.

Wes' face went blank and his mind started to wander as he tried to cover his tracks.

"We're dressing up to serve the kids dinner on Saturday night," he finally said.

"You liar!" Jenny smiled, knowing something was up.

"You got me! It's not for the retreat," Wes admitted. "I'm not even going on the retreat."

Jenny took a deep breath, waiting to hear what Wes would say next.

"Actually, I'm heading to Santa Barbara for the weekend," he said.

"Were you planning on telling me about this?" Jenny's tone changed to frustration.

"Well, yeah!" Wes replied. "It would be difficult to keep it from you when we're both driving up the 101 to Santa Barbara! I think you might get very suspicious when we're out to dinner in 'The Barbara!'" Or when we check into The Inn of the Spanish Garden."

"What?" Jenny's mouth curled up at both ends.

Wes got up from his shirt-folding and moved toward Jenny.

"Well, so much for surprises!" he said. "I had it all lined up, too!"

He paused.

"I feel like I lost my rhythm with you when we moved here. I really want that back. I never felt like I pushed you out, but it hit me: You got drowned out! I'm *that* pastor, the one who allows the urgent to replace his first love."

Jenny's eyes welled up.

"Anyway, I was hoping this weekend would give us time to talk through some things," he said.

"I can't believe we're going to Santa Barbara, and you're not going on the middle school retreat!"

"I'd be just a figurehead this weekend," Wes assured her. "I have so much to talk to you about."

"I find that difficult to believe!" she replied.

For the next few months, Wes mulled over Britt's steps and Doug's story. He told Jenny what he was thinking about, but no one else. Jenny pushed him to share the steps with the youth staff. She was convinced the steps could transform students' spiritual lives. She said she had evidence to prove it.

Jenny led a small group of senior girls. They were her joy. Most of them had been in the group since seventh grade. One Sunday night Jenny asked the group about spiritual questioning and doubt. The response was overwhelming. Girl after girl shared things they felt they couldn't talk about in church. Their relief over being able to talk openly about spiritual doubts fueled Jenny's resolve to encourage Wes to implement the steps at Coastline.

Wes was less than convinced.

"That doesn't prove anything," he argued. "Those girls love everything you do! They've loved you since the day you took over the group. They even meet together when you're gone! You have the easy group. Now if it were my guys—that would be a different story. My group is like a house of cards. One mistake, one criticism, one burp, and the whole thing falls apart."

"Why don't you just give it a shot?" Jenny asked.

Wes ticked off the reasons on his fingers.

"Let's see—the staff and leaders might misunderstand the steps. Students might get pushed in the wrong spiritual direction. I'll be put in the position of defending a strategy I'm not convinced of yet. Then there's the issue of timing. Trying to do something this big at the end of the school year doesn't make sense. Plus, the numbers have been steady lately, so this probably isn't the time to shake things up.

"I just need to make sure my leadership is nice and tight right now," Wes continued. "No surprises. Until I can verbalize it, teach it, prove it—"

"And place a nice bow on top of it," Jenny added.

"Right," Wes agreed. "Until I can do those things, the steps will have to stay in the research and development part of my brain. Think about it. Would Microsoft bring a product to market if it hadn't been proven, tested, and had all the bugs worked out of it? Okay, bad example!"

The turning point came one Sunday when Wes was meeting with his small group of sophomore guys. They were knee-deep in a series on prayer, no pun intended. Despite Wes' best efforts, his guys seemed uninterested in the topic. Getting them to engage with the material was like getting them to take medicine.

The group started their time together with *hang time*, a few minutes during which they took turns checking in with each other to see how the previous week had gone. Wes had introduced hang time as a way of preventing stragglers from missing anything important. But it had taken on a life of its own. The guys usually pushed to see how far they could extend hang time before Wes turned the conversation to spiritual things.

On this particular Sunday the boys were especially scattered. They were laughing and joking, more intent in their ridiculousness than ever. Wes tried a number of times to have them each check in but was derailed at every opportunity. Wes' frustration grew and he became increasingly short with the boys. And still they kept messing around.

Finally Wes' aggravation got the better of him.

"I'll give you 10 bucks if you can name one time—*one time*—God answered one of your prayers," he announced as he reached for his wallet.

There was a brief pause in the room, and then the responses began.

"I got a puppy when I was eight after I prayed," Will said. "We even named it Easter. Now where's my 10 bucks?"

Wes shook his head, "Your parents bought him; no good."

"I prayed for a basketball game we had earlier this year," Zander said. "It was a big game, and we won."

"Fifty-fifty, no dice!" Wes said.

The guys pled their cases for the next few minutes. David even called his mom on his cell phone to prove his aunt was free of her cancer. But he was disqualified when he admitted it was more his whole family praying than him specifically.

"For 10 dollars it has to start with you and end with you," Wes announced.

As the mood of the group turned more reflective, an idea occurred to Wes. *Instigate questions.*

"Have you ever prayed and begged God for something and still had it not happen?" he asked.

"Do I get the 10 bucks?" David countered.

"We'll see."

David told a story about a girl he really liked in eighth grade and the deal he tried to make with God if she would like him. The guys laughed as they tried to guess who the girl was.

"Jared, what about you?" Wes asked.

"Nothing really," Jared said.

"Matt, have you ever had God not answer a prayer?"

"Yeah," Matt said in a low voice. "My grandfather got really sick, and I prayed—my whole family prayed—and he still died."

The room went quiet. Wes felt a powerful urge to offer an explanation to Matt. But that urge was overruled by another thought. *Just instigate!* he told himself.

"So does God answer prayer, or do we take whatever happens and make it fit our faith?" Wes asked. "If your grandfather is healed, God did it. If he dies, God took him home and relieved his suffering."

The boys had never heard Wes talk like that. They were waiting for him to answer, but he sat quiet until Zander spoke up.

"I've thought about that a lot," Zander admitted. "How do we know if God is really there? I think he is, but then sometimes I think maybe I'm making the whole thing up. You know, talking to myself."

Zander's honesty opened the door for others to share. Many of the other guys agreed with Zander. They'd felt the same way, thought the same thoughts. Another student, Chris, said he always knew God was there when he prayed.

Wes played referee, making sure that what was shared wasn't quickly forgotten, and everyone had a chance to share.

"How do we know we're not making up God in our heads? How do you know God is there?" Wes asked.

Will spoke up.

"Okay, I think some of you know I have dyslexia," he divulged. "I've asked God to take it away and make me normal, but nothing has ever happened. So I wonder if God answers, and why he made me like this."

No one expected that out of Will. Normally he was the first one to try to push things off track. He usually said little to nothing when the talk came to spiritual things. For his part, Wes had no idea Will was dyslexic. Wes was suddenly getting a much clearer picture of his small group guys.

Time was up just as things were starting to get rolling. For the first time in a while, Wes wished he had more time with his guys.

The switch had been flipped.

Wes texted Britt on his way home: "Jedi, need to talk. Ready for the chi tea!"

In the following weeks, Wes' sophomore guys had more amazing moments of honesty, hardship, and horsing around. Wes watched excitedly as the steps spurred conversations he'd seldom had with students. He found himself spending significant time following up with each of the guys individually.

That's when he realized the steps were changing the way he thought of youth ministry—not to mention his role as a youth pastor.

Wes and Britt continued to meet throughout the summer. Wes had a growing desire to introduce his staff and leaders to the steps so they could corporately change the culture of their youth group. Before he did that, though, he scheduled a meeting with Britt to talk over the program changes.

Once they were seated Wes opened his backpack and pulled out several multicolored folders. The one on top was labeled "Scope and Sequence." Inside was a neatly prepared outline of the year's youth group talks, designed specifically to go hand-in-glove with a spiral chart that explained the new program emphasis for the Coastline youth ministry.

"What's this obsession with programming?" Britt asked as he looked over the material. "This is awesome overkill. I love all the colors."

"Well, I tried to make changes and still fit them inside the Coastline strategy," Wes explained.

"You mean the same language?" Britt asked.

"Same language, same colors..." Wes began.

"Same colors?" Britt asked.

"Everything we do in evangelism for the church is orange. Discipleship is green. Worship is—"

"Got it," Britt said. "The color-driven church. Sweet!"

"Okay, I just want to make sure I have my bases covered when I present it to the staff and other pastors."

"I understand," Britt replied. "So have you told anyone else about your plan or about the steps?"

"Obviously I told Jenny—and my admin Bonnie, who helped come up with a lot of this," Wes explained.

"What about the rest of your staff?" Britt pressed. "Have you said anything to them?"

"A little bit," Wes replied. His plan during the summer was to have one-on-one conversations to test the water. Every conversation had been different, however. He had to share more with Bonnie, but that turned out to be a windfall. Bonnie thought it was brave and spent considerable time fleshing out the program design.

"Looks like you have it all figured out," Britt said as he handed back Wes' folder.

"No way!" Wes exclaimed. "I'm overdoing it because I'm scared the whole thing might blow up! So I want proof that I was thoughtful when I crashed this ministry." They both laughed as Wes grabbed the invisible controls of a nose-diving airplane.

"What are you most afraid of?" Britt asked.

"Well, numbers going down, leaders disagreeing with me, losing my job," Wes replied in his most sarcastic tone. "You know, the usual."

"Well, maybe instead of trying to change your program, you should just try to change your leaders," Britt suggested. "It's not about program, but what's behind the program. Rearranging your furniture or getting a new house doesn't help you raise better children."

"But if you have no kitchen in your house, eating will be difficult," Wes replied.

"Is it your program you're worried about or your people?" Britt asked. "Your programs are good, better than anything I have done. But the feel is the content."

"What?" Wes asked.

"The feel is the content," Britt repeated. "What you're really teaching is what students feel, the vibe your youth group throws."

"Another California touchy-feely thing," Wes said as he rolled his eyes.

"Think about it," Britt urged. "You know this is true with students. You can tell students you love them every time you get together, but if your leaders are overly strict or just mean, what will they believe? Remember, young students especially are more relationally driven than intellectually driven."

"Okay, another thing to think about," Wes said with a chuckle.

"Let me ask you another question," Britt said. "Who decides the flavor of your group?"

Me? No, the students? The leaders? Wes thought to himself. He didn't give Britt an answer. He needed to think about it some more.

Britt interrupted his thoughts.

"Can I tell you about a dream I had?"

"Okay," Wes responded. He knew enough about Britt to know that it should be interesting.

"I'm throwing a party in my dream and people start showing up at my house," Britt explained. "The first person to arrive is No. 6, Julius Erving. You know? Dr J. Then one after another people keep showing up. C.S. Lewis, John MacArthur, Bill Hybels, Billy Graham, my high school pastor Bill Zipp, N. T. Wright, Jerry Falwell, Mother Teresa, Chuck Colson, Corrie ten Boom. I can't believe all these people are in my house!"

"You throw quite a party!" Wes laughed. "When people come back from the dead to party with you, you've arrived, my man!"

"No, I'm panicking!" Britt explained. "I keep trying to steer people away from each other. Mother Teresa and Jerry Falwell are talking. That can't be good! Hybels, MacArthur, and James Dunn are on my couch talking with Scot McKnight about the Cubs. Anyway, I'm trying to rearrange everyone when I start to realize everyone's happy and getting along. And I mean getting along swimmingly!"

"So you're in heaven?" Wes asked.

"Dude, didn't you hear me? How could you be in heaven when people are talking about the Cubs? No, I realize that all those people in my house are all the people who've influenced my faith and ministry. In life, they might not seem to get along. But in my head, in my theology, they get along great!"

"So you're saying I should have a party?" Wes joked.

"What I'm driving at is that your leaders might not agree with you—and that's not all bad! Still invite them to the party. If you're honest with yourself, you'll realize they probably don't agree with you on everything right now. I'll bet you have a charismatic hiding somewhere on your staff. It might be a healthy thing for your students to know that. I know it goes against the leadership color scheme, but the body of Christ is made up of different parts. Your students need many different voices from your staff."

Wes liked Britt's dream illustration so much he shared it with Jenny later that evening. Then they both wrote down who would be at their parties.

"You know, Wes," Jenny said as they compared lists, "this would be a great exercise for our leaders to do."

"Imagine how much it would bring to light!" Wes said excitedly.

Two weeks later, Wes got together with Britt again. "I think you're in my head!" he told Britt.

"I am? Maybe it's just my Mr. Miyagi Karate Kid vibe."

"Easy, '80s Man," Wes said. "It's ironic, though, that since we started talking, everything's changed and nothing's changed."

Britt looked perplexed. "How so?"

"Well, I still have the same boss, still work with the same kids, still deal with the same parents, still manage the same staff, and still work in a big church where expectations are still high!"

"So what's changed?" Britt asked.

"I think my focus is starting to shift," Wes explained. "All this conversation about the steps has me thinking more about how spiritual transformation happens and less about other stuff."

"Such as?"

"Stuff like programming—trying to impress my senior pastor, parents, and even myself! I think it's just easy to assume that when students are excited about showing up to a program, it must be a sign of spiritual growth. Go down that road and pretty soon numbers start to be the key measure of success. I think at Coastline we measure just about everything *but* spiritual growth."

"So how do you change that?" Britt asked.

"You tell me!" Wes said. "I know that shooting for numbers is the way *not* to get them! Students know when that's your goal. You can't hide it. I think they can actually smell it!"

"Does your senior pastor smell it?" Britt asked.

"I don't think Richard smells much from our ministry *but* numbers," Wes replied. "That's the rock and the hard place. Feeling pushed for numbers and knowing kids hate being targeted! It's frustrating to feel you're being evaluated one-dimensionally."

"The obvious question is: Have you talked to Richard about it?" Britt asked.

"Not really," Wes said, "because—thanks to you—I just figured out that I'm frustrated! I think if I can come up with better gauges, he would embrace them. But until then... it's rear ends in seats! That's why I want to make sure my programming is airtight, so the measures will be, too!"

"Well, I think it's healthy for you to make sure you and Richard are on the same page," Britt said. "That's your responsibility if you're moving in this new direction."

"You're right!" Wes said smiling at the thought of his new autonomy. "*I'm* the one responsible for letting Richard and the rest of the church know what page I'm on!"

"And our conversation about leaders?" Britt asked.

"I should have already had this conversation with them," Wes admitted. "I need to bring them into the conversation we've been having. What are your leadership meetings like with your volunteers at Trinity?"

"They're pretty cool," Britt said with a grin. "Not because of anything I do. We spend most of our time telling stories."

"Stories?" Wes asked.

"Stories about students and what's going on in their lives, the dynamic in the small groups," Britt explained. "I find that stories communicate better than I ever could. I really like that everyone can participate, and even the newest people can add something. Our leaders don't like to miss our times together. The story connects them together."

"Connects them? How does it connect them?" Wes responded.

"In my early career I found it was easy to give leaders jobs. 'Stand by the door, make sure no one gets out!' But those leaders never stayed very long. Then I gave leaders the best roles, the best kids, the best cabins at camp. That helped us retain leaders and made them feel important. One day I realized I trusted them with what was most important—the students—but I didn't trust them as much with our time together as adults."

"What did you do?" Wes asked.

"I told them."

"You told them you didn't trust them?"

"No, I told them I *did* trust them and kept asking them to take more ownership of our leaders' time," Britt said. "My thought was that I needed to replace myself at every level so no part of the youth ministry is dependent on me, my personality, or my gifts. Within four to six months, the leaders told me the highlight of our meetings was the story time about students. They went from feeling connected to a few leaders and students to feeling connected to many. The stories teach powerfully, too—more than I imagined. So that's become our thing."

The more Britt talked, the more convinced Wes became about what he needed to do.

It was a Saturday morning in September. The volunteers for middle and high school ministry at Coastline had gathered for an all-day kickoff training time. New faces and the usual suspects were all there eating breakfast.

Wes welcomed them.

"This year we're going to try some different things. I honestly don't know where we'll end up, but I think it'll be good," Wes stated. "I think it will be *very* good. God has had me on this journey over the last year here at Coastline and is shaping me in some different ways. But I'll share more about that another time. This morning I thought we'd start by hearing from someone who has something I think we all need to hear."

To the surprise of many, Doug Rothschild walked from the back of the room to share his story and launch a new vision in Coastline's youth ministry.

A FEW LAST THOUGHTS

For most of my ministry life, I've worked with middle schoolers. It's been wonderful! They've taught me so many things about life and ministry. My weaknesses, strengths, and motivations were all exposed when I began working with 12-year-olds. There's just nowhere to hide with them! They're able to figure out and expose who you really are. They're honest to a fault and pick up none of the social cues that make life as a grownup easy. They're so awkwardly fun!

The steps mentioned in the story have been unknowingly taught to me by my students over the years. They desire for adults to lovingly pursue them, to listen to their thoughts, and to help them imagine the world they're moving into. They need to have the freedom to struggle, doubt, and experience the crisis that is developmentally built into this time of life.

These thoughts are not revolutionary. I think all of human history can attest to a teenager's ability to create drama. Somehow it took me years to learn to appreciate it. Instead of putting up with crisis or questioning, hoping for it to end with the onset of adulthood, it actually started to occur to me that the crisis and questioning were part of God's design. The steps come from the desire to embrace this part of their life journey.

The steps as I've described them are sequential and linear—a simple and predictable package. But we know nothing about teenagers is sequential or linear. The steps in my mind all overlap each other in a 3-D atom-like matrix of swirling goodness. They happen in order, out of order, and at the same time. My strategy in this book is to make them pronounced so they stand out. So please don't overanalyze the order.

One of the questions I talked over with friends was: Does crisis bring doubt or does doubt bring crisis? I had supersmart people tell me it's crisis that brings doubt and other supersmart people say it's doubt that creates crisis. I see both happening in the narrative of Scripture. My life and ministry with students back this up, too. The important point here is the embracing of doubt and tension, not the order. Students' lives are messy. When we get involved beyond a superficial level, we get messy and so does our process.

Even though the steps aren't always sequential, I believe they're cyclical. The steps are a constant for discovering the presence of God. When I came to faith in high school, the model of discipleship that was given to me was mainly informational. I was told knowing Scripture and mastering the biblical languages would lead me to a deeper understanding of God's heart.

Though I benefited tremendously from my journey, at times I found myself acting more as a biblical attorney than a pastor—parsing Greek verbs to prove my point or theology. I have to admit that I was—and still am—quite gnostic in my faith. I allow the focus of my walk with God to emphasize intellectual assent. For a comprehensive list of my issues, please ask my wife, Pam, who knows me best. The point is that questions, doubt, and tension accomplish what information alone could not: They humble me. I find that each new year, each new friendship, each new life stage has me starting over with Jesus. I start asking him different questions and off I go! The process of questioning and doubt overlap, but it's a constant for our growth. By God's good grace I hope that process will last all my life.

More than ever, I believe ministering to the next generation is beyond essential. I'm convinced student ministry is the safe reformation in the church. If we as youth workers drop the ball, the church will feel the negative effects immediately—as well as 10, 15, and 20 years from now. Without drawing on the hyperbole of statistics, I will say that now is a crucial time for youth ministry to lead the church. The voice of young people is our good hope.

Our society has dramatically changed over the last 20 years of my ministry. We have less and less shared culture compared with the decades before. Not long ago most Americans got their news from the same place: Walter Cronkite. We watched the same shows and listened to much of the same music. The most popular weekly TV show today wouldn't have cracked the Top 10 in the '70s. We all know how the Internet has changed things. The world is flat, and information is doubling at the speed of light...or something like that.

Why bring this up?

It's not just to illustrate why big evangelism events are less effective than they used to be—the fact that one speaker's message covers and connects to fewer people now. Students today are keenly aware of more than just their own cultural story. When I came to Christ as a high school student back in the day, I faced just one story and one question: Am I willing to follow Jesus? I never questioned that question. Even as an unchurched kid, I never doubted the shared scriptural story of God. Students today question the question—even the students in our churches.

Questioning and doubt are crucial for discipleship because of this new paradigm. Teens today filter through gobs of information each day. If we're going to effectively disciple them, we need to do more than give them our information. We also need to help them sift through the rest of the information (and misinformation) they're exposed to. The steps are a framework for offering them the kind of guidance they're looking for. I realize that for many of us, this approach feels strange because the starting place is so different from ours. But to demand that a student start where we did—or even assume that a student *can* start where we did—can produce a disastrous result: A marginalized faith.

Effective transformation happens when God's story and a student's story connect. To make that happen, we must take the time to delve deep into a student's life. We must also have the humility to recognize that God's story is bigger than us. My best moments as a youth pastor have come when I realize God's voice is loud in a student's life—louder than our youth group, louder than our leaders, louder than me.

I hope this book encourages us as youth workers to create systems that necessitate communication. In no way do I desire to put forward a program to follow. I know effective youth ministries that are as different as New York- and

Chicago-style pizzas. Don't get me started. I believe it's the ethos behind the programs that makes the most profound impact on young people's long-term spiritual growth. The steps are my best effort to encourage us as youth workers to rethink our very posture with students.

I hope this book has caused you to think, to talk to your students and other youth ministers—and even to find points of disagreement with me.

If it has...congratulations!

My Jedi mind trick worked.

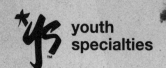

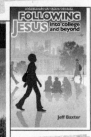

NATIONAL YOUTH WORKERS CONVENTION

youth specialties

You find yourself in a new conversation every day...

COME FIND YOURSELF IN OURS.